DATE DUE

JANUA LINGUARUM

STUDIA MEMORIAE
NICOLAI VAN WIJK DEDICATA

edenda curat
C. H. VAN SCHOONEVELD
Indiana University

Series Minor, 187

SEMANTICS
AND
COMPREHENSION

by

Herbert H. Clark

1976
MOUTON
THE HAGUE · PARIS

ISBN 90 279 3384 7

Printed in the Netherlands

TABLE OF CONTENTS

PREFACE

In the Fall of 1969 Professor Thomas A. Sebeok invited me to contribute a chapter on language comprehension to Volume 12 of *Current Trends in Linguistics*. I accepted his invitation with the thought of writing a 50-page review of the basic psychological studies in comprehension. But I was hoist with my own petard. As it happened, William Chase and I had just completed a dozen or so experiments in the two short months before I left Carnegie-Mellon University in the Spring of 1969, experiments on how one judges whether a sentence is true or false of a picture. I knew some of the literature on negation, and since we had used sentences with negatives, I knew vaguely that the model we had come up with for our task was consistent with what I knew of the literature. But in preparing for the chapter I was about to write, I dug into this literature in earnest and was astounded by what I found. Not only did our model fit the studies I encountered, but it also made sense of the numerous conflicting results in that literature. As initial evidence for our model, the negation literature seemed even more than I could have hoped for.

I should have stopped there. But because the sentences Chase and I had used contained locatives, I dug just as earnestly into the psychological literature on locatives, and I was just as pleased with what I found there. And because this literature dealt as much with transitive verbs as it did with locatives, I was enticed into the rather large literature on actives and passives, and that turned out to be rewarding for my general viewpoint too. And because I had just published work on deductive reasoning using comparatives, I felt obliged to round out my treatment of the general model of comprehension with a discussion of the comparatives literature. Along the way, of course, various empirical studies suggested themselves, and I began to add my own experiments to the list I had to account for. By the time I finished writing in October of 1970, the short 50-page chapter I had envisioned had exploded into a 250-page monograph.

The present form of the monograph is exactly as I finished it in the Fall of 1970, except for up-dated references to the papers that have come out subsequently. The empirical and theoretical work derived from this monograph, of course, has gone on since 1970, both in my own laboratory and elsewhere, and can be found mainly in the pages of the *Journal of Verbal Learning and Verbal Behavior, Cognitive Psychology, Cognition, Psychological Review*, and the *Journal of Experimental Psychology*. Nevertheless, the basic viewpoint expressed here is as valid today as it was in 1970, and because many investigators are still unaware of the coherence of the empirical support for this point, the monograph itself, I believe, is as valuable today as it was in 1970. I can only hope that this monograph may bring to some investigators a new appreciation for the psychological literature on comprehension, its strengths and its weaknesses, and that some will find the viewpoint expressed here valuable in their own theory and research.

I wish to acknowledge my indebtedness to William G. Chase, of Carnegie-Mellon University, for his close collaboration in the work on negation that triggered this monograph. And I am also indebted to a number of students working with me at the time who played a truly central role in the development of the present monograph: Patricia Carpenter, Marcel Just, Carole Offir, Frederick Springston, and Neil Stillings. Finally, I wish to thank Eve V. Clark for her comments on the theory and manuscript throughout the writing of this monograph.

Stanford California,   HERBERT H. CLARK
March 1974

SEMANTICS AND COMPREHENSION

HERBERT H. CLARK *

INTRODUCTION

Comprehension is fundamental to the study of language. In their investigations, most linguists have relied heavily on what people understand a sentence to mean, and their theories have been designed in part to account for these so-called 'linguistic intuitions'. On the other hand, psycholinguists have more often been interested in the *difficulties* people have in understanding sentences, and their theories have usually been designed to account for these difficulties. More generally, while linguists have usually been concerned with the *end-product* of comprehension, psychologists have been concerned with the *process* of comprehension. The present chapter reports on an attempt to develop a general theory of comprehension that includes selected aspects of both the process and end-product of comprehension. The purpose of section 1 is simply to outline the theory, its assumptions, and its justification. The purpose of sections 2 through 5 is to apply this theory quite specifically to four basic constructions in English — namely, negatives, locatives, comparatives, and actives and passives — and to demonstrate that the theory is adequate to account for the major psychological (and linguistic) evidence available on these constructions. Although the theory is certainly not complete at the present time, it is useful in the following respects: (1) it makes sense of the previous experimental work on comprehension in a unified framework; (2) it points out the gaps in our knowledge and theory of comprehension; and (3) it provides a unified framework for future empirical studies and theories in comprehension.

Comprehension will be approached mainly as a problem in semantics, in the broadest sense of this word. The first problem of the theory is to characterize what it is that a person knows of the meaning of a sentence once he has 'comprehended' the sentence. This is what I will call the *representation problem*, and it will be our first concern in the application of the theory to the various English constructions. The second problem is to characterize the processes by which a person uses the 'meaning' of a sentence to do other things — e.g. decide whether the sentence is true or false, answer questions about that sentence, carry out commands

* I am indebted to Eve V. Clark for her helpful comments on the manuscript of this chapter.

made by the sentence, and so on. This will involve us in the *processing problem*. The processing problem, however, is very closely tied to the representation problem, for the method by which the semantic representation of a sentence is processed depends critically on the form the representation itself is assumed to take in the mind. The strategy in the present chapter is therefore to characterize the semantic representation of a sentence as completely as possible and then to investigate the subsequent processes that are required in using this representation in sentence verification, question answering, instruction following, and the like.

1. REPRESENTATION

1.1 *The Problem*

The first order of business is to characterize what it is that a person has come to know in reading or listening to a sentence. This information, normally called the meaning of the sentence, is to be contrasted with judgments one can make about that meaning — e.g. is it true? is it silly? is it acceptable? is it nonsensical? and so on. The semantic representation — or simply the representation — of a sentence refers to a notation that characterizes the meaning of that sentence, what a person knows of the content of that sentence.

1.11 *The deep structure assumption*

The semantic representation of a sentence, I assume, is equivalent to, or closely related to, the linguistic deep structure of the sentence. By using the term 'deep structure', I do not mean to pre-judge the current linguistic controversies as to whether language is best accounted for by a deep structure plus semantic interpretation (as in Chomsky 1965), by a system of generative semantics (as in Lakoff 1971; McCawley 1968; Postal 1970), by a case grammar (as in Fillmore 1968; Anderson 1971), or by something else. Rather, 'deep structure' is meant to refer to an adequate linguistic representation of the underlying structure of a sentence, whatever that will turn out to be. In the present chapter, we will need to refer only to linguistic facts and representations that ought to be acceptable to all variants of current generative grammar.

The a priori justification for the deep structure assumption is quite straightforward. One requirement of a general theory of comprehension is that semantic representations conform to two constraints: (1) they must satisfy all linguistic intuitions, or linguistic facts, about what a sentence means, whether it is acceptable, semantically anomalous, ungrammatical, or whatever, what its accurate paraphrases are, and so on; (2) it must also be compatible with a process that accepts a semantic representation and manipulates it appropriately to answer questions, follow directions, decide on issues of truth and falsity, and so on. Since the goals of linguistic theory are simply those of (1), we automatically satisfy the first condition by making the deep structure assumption — at least to the limit of present day linguistic theory. In contrast, very little has been said previously about the second condition: that is one of the main goals of this chapter. To put it another way, the linguistic facts at our disposal are both far more extensive and far more systematic than our knowledge about the subsequent processes that make use of semantic representations. Thus it seems prudent to begin with the best qualified semantic representations derived from linguistic theory and to explore the possible 'mental processes' that can be built onto them to account for question answering, sentence verification, instruction following, and the like. The success of the present chapter to a large extent is due to the fact that this strategy has been followed as closely as possible. As will be seen, the strategy enables us to make some very strong generalizations about the mental processes that manipulate semantic representations.

To put the justification in another way, the claim is being made that linguistic deep structure accurately represents what people know once they have 'comprehended' a sentence. In advance of many other concrete examples to be given in subsequent sections, consider the negative sentence *John isn't happy*. Linguistically, this sentence is composed roughly of two propositions, *John is happy* and *It is false*, with the first embedded within the second, as in *that John is happy is false*. The semantic representation of this sentence might be coded as follows: *((John is happy) is false)*. Such a representation characterizes much of what a person understands the sentence to mean: (1) that *happy* applies to *John* and not to something else; (2) that *false* applies to the proposition that John is happy, not simply to *John* or to something else; (3) that to show that the sentence is true, it is enough to show that the embedded proposition *(John is happy)* is false; and so on. In addition, it will be shown in section 2 that the two propositions, one embedded within the other, are essential to the psychological model that accounts for the latencies with which people are able to verify negative sentences like this one. In short, there is evidence — both linguistic and psychological — that the linguistic deep structure does accurately characterize what people understand a sentence to mean.

There are limitations, however, on how literally we should accept the deep structure assumption, for it could be taken in either a strong or a weak form. In its strongest form, the assumption is that a person who has comprehended a sentence 'knows' every detail represented in linguistic deep structure. In a weaker form, the assumption is that whatever it is that a person 'knows' of a sentence is *consistent* with linguistic deep structure, but he does not necessarily represent all or even most of the details of deep structure each time he comprehends a sentence. It seems highly unlikely that the strong form will be correct, though it is quite plausible that some version of the weak form will. This implies that the linguistic deep structure contains many details that a listener might well pass over and leave unrepresented on any particular occasion; nevertheless, those details that he does represent must be consistent with deep structure, since otherwise the listener will be said to have misunderstood the sentence. This point is best made with an example. Consider the sentence *John thought to himself, 'Mary has just come into the kitchen'*. If the listener were interested only in knowing where Mary was, he might well ignore the presupposition of *come*, that John must be in the kitchen (cf. Fillmore 1967a), and represent *come* simply as 'move'. But if the listener were interested in knowing where *John* was, he could not ignore that presupposition; he would have to represent *come* as 'move' plus its presupposition, i.e. as 'move toward John'. It is difficult to assert a priori that the listener will always represent the presupposition of *come*, since it is easy to imagine a listener who is quite unable to say where John was, even though the information was in the original sentence the listener had read and 'understood' a moment before. The assumption is, however, that whenever the listener does represent the presupposition of *come*, he will do so in a way consistent with the linguistic representation of *come* in its context.

1.2 *The Processing Problem*

The listener is assumed to construct a semantic representation for each sentence he understands, and that representation is assumed to serve as the basis for all further processes that require the comprehended information. This brings us to the processing problem: just what processes does the listener use on semantic representations in order to verify sentences, answer questions, and follow instructions appropriately? For this purpose, I have formalized the complete representation and processing problems in a specific yet easily generalizable schema or format. The schema is not an arbitrary one, for it has empirical consequences that can be tested in any comprehension task that it is applied to. As we will see, the schema itself is given considerable empirical support in the literature to be examined later.

1.21 *The four-stage schema*

The assumption is that most 'comprehension' tasks can be broken down into four identifiable stages (cf. Clark 1969a; Clark and Chase 1972). Consider the so-called verification task in which the experimental subject is given a sentence and a picture and is asked whether the sentence is true or false of the picture. At Stage 1, the subject is presumed to encode the sentence — i.e. to construct a semantic representation for the sentence. At Stage 2, the subject codes the picture in a representation that is in the same format as the sentence. At Stage 3, the subject carries out a series of mental operations that compare his representation of the sentence with that of the picture to determine whether they are synonymous or not. And at Stage 4, the subject takes the outcome of the Stage 3 comparison operations and converts that outcome — e.g. *true* — into the vocalization 'true', into the press of a button marked 'true' or into whatever response is appropriate. So the process includes four stages — a sentence representation stage, a picture representation stage, a comparison stage, and a response stage. The four stages must be serially ordered: the sentence and picture must be represented before their representations can be compared; the comparison stage has to be complete before the response stage can realize the outcome of the comparison stage; however, the two representation stages could be in either order, depending on the task requirements.

The four-stage process just given is applicable to comprehension tasks of all kinds with minor alterations in the stages. First, let us examine the verification task again in a little more detail. Assume that a subject is required to verify the sentence *A is above B* against a picture of an A above a B. Hypothetically, the process might appear as in:

1   Stage 1: Represent sentence as *(A above B)*
     Stage 2: Represent picture as *(A above B)*
     Stage 3: Compare *(A above B)* with *(A above B)* for synomymy
     Stage 4: Produce the response 'true'

Although it is critical to know how the sentence and picture are represented at Stages 1 and 2, the heart of the task is the Stage 3 comparison process. It must be expanded into a set of mental operations that compare the Stage 1 and 2 representations piece by piece, since in much more complex examples, the comparison will not be as obvious or simple as in this example. Indeed, the main proposals of the present chapter are concerned with the Stage 3 comparison operations and their effects on the latency of the Stage 4 response. I will return to the Stage 3 mental operations later.

In contrast, consider a question-answering task, such as *If John killed Harry, then who died?* In this case, the four stages would appear as in:

2   Stage 1: Represent premise as *(John caused (Harry die))*
     Stage 2: Represent question as *(X die)*
     Stage 3: Compare *(John caused (Harry die))* and *(X die):* find *X*
     Stage 4: Produce the response 'Harry'

Stages 1 and 2 in 2 are identical in format to the same stages in the verification task; if the same sentences had been used, the representations would be identical. Stage 4 is also the same except for the specific response. There is a difference, however, at Stage 3. Whereas Stage 3 simply matched the two representations for identity in the verification task, it must match representations and pick out an *X* in the question answering task. It will become clear that this is a minor difference, for the matching operations are carried out in the same way in both tasks.

In the next task to be illustrated, the subject is given a page full of digits and is required to carry out the instruction *Cross out all even numbers*. This task might be represented as 3:

3   Stage 1: Represent instruction as *(you cross out X (if (X is even)))*
     Stage 2: Represent the current digit (e.g. 8) as *(8 is even)*
     Stage 3: Compare representations from Stages 1 and 2
     Stage 4: Produce response consistent with *(you cross out 8)*

This task, in fact, contains a verification process within it. One can think of the Stage 3 comparison as having two parts: in the first, the subject compares the *if*-clause of the instruction with the *(8 is even)* exactly as in the verification task; in the second, the subject 'attaches' the outcome *(true)* of this comparison to the main clause of the instruction to produce the representation *(true (you cross out 8))* from which the response is made at Stage 4. So although this task is superficially quite different from the verification task in **1**, it can be conceptualized in almost identical stages and comparison processes.

The four-stage schema, as applied to the verification, question-answering, and instruction-following tasks, is more than just a convenient conceptualization of these tasks. Underlying the schema are three very important empirical claims. The first claim is that a sentence is represented (understood) in the same way no matter what the task is. Stages 1 and 2 are in principle identical in form for the verification, question-answering, and instruction-following tasks. The sentence *A is above B,* for example, would be represented as *(A above B)* at Stage 1 no matter what the task. Although this claim is open to empirical test, the evidence available (to be presented later) suggests that this claim is indeed true. The second empirical claim is that the representation stages (Stages 1 and 2) are separate from the comparison stage (Stage 3), which in turn is separate from the production of the response (Stage 4). Furthermore, the representation stages, the comparison stage, and the response stage must be carried out in this order. I will present evidence later that supports this empirical claim. The third and final claim is that the comparison stages (Stage 3) in the three tasks all have something in common: they work from the semantic representations of sentences, carry out comparisons and manipulations on these underlying representations, and eventually produce outcomes (like *true* or *false*) that serve as the basis for Stage 4 response. One part of this claim is that these comparison stages do *not* operate directly on the surface structure of the sentences, on mental images, or on other 'uninterpreted' representations. Evidence for this claim will be considered later. A second part of this claim is that comparisons are made by checking for the IDENTITY of various parts of the Stage 1 and 2 representations. These claims are part of an assumption I have previously called the PRINCIPLE OF CONGRUENCE (Clark 1969a).

1.22 *The principle of congruence*

Imagine that a person has read and understood the sentence *John killed Harry.* Now we might ask him, *Who died?*, a question that is simple enough for the listener to answer. Our listener knows, roughly, that he must find a term which, when it replaces the *who* in *Who died?*, will make the corresponding declarative sentence true. One possible way to do this would be to match surface structures — to see if *died* can be found in the original sentence and, if so, to take the term immediately preceding *died* as the correct answer. This, of course, will not work here, and it would not work even in sentences that explicitly contain *died*, as in *The person who died was Harry, Harry — according to John — died with his boots on*, etc. etc. To answer *Who died?*, therefore, this listener must search not through surface structure, but through deep structure, seeking congruence between selected parts of the semantic representations of the premise and the question. *Who died?* can be answered once *John killed Harry* is represented as (*John caused* (*Harry die*)) and *Who died?* as (*X die*). Then (*X die*) can be matched with (*Harry die*), *X* replaced by *Harry*, and the question answered by 'Harry'.

This is one line of reasoning that led to the PRINCIPLE OF CONGRUENCE, which asserts simply that the Stage 3 comparison operations work to make underlying representations completely congruent with each other. The basic operation, then, is the match. (*X die*) is matched against (*Harry die*); the two representations are found to be identical except for the mismatch of *X* and *Harry*; and so *X* is replaced by *Harry* in accordance with the requirements of the task. Thus the answer 'Harry died' (or in elliptical form 'Harry did' or simply 'Harry') is fully congruent with a complete part of the semantic representation of the sentence *John killed Harry*. To take another illustration, the sentence *A is above B*, represented as (*A above B*), might be verified against a picture represented as (*B below A*). Since these two representations are not congruent, an additional operation is required to transform one of the two representations, e.g. (*B below A*) into (*A above B*), in order to make them congruent. After this transformation, the two representations are completely congruent, an identity match will succeed, and the sentence can be pronounced 'true' of the picture.

The principle of congruence has several important theoretical and empirical consequences. First, the principle provides the basis for constructing a set of Stage 3 comparison operations that will correctly solve the task at hand. Without such a principle, it is impossible to specify just how Stage 3 would go about deciding, for example, whether (*A above B*) and (*B below A*) are synonymous or not. In more complex cases to be considered later, the Stage 3 operations would be quite ad hoc without such a principle. Second, the principle implies that certain comparisons should be more difficult than others. In particular, whenever there is incongruence, an additional manipulation operation is required of Stage 3 in order to bring the two representations into congruence. If it is assumed simply that each of these additional operations takes time to perform, tasks with incongruent semantic representations should take longer, or elicit more errors, than tasks with congruent semantic representations. I will use this particular argument time and again to make predictions about response latencies in verification, question-answering, and instruction-following tasks. In particular, this second implication has been shown to hold very closely for the verification of negative sentences (Clark and Chase 1972), a fact that will be discussed at length in section 2.

1.3 *Recapitulation*

In section 1, then, I have outlined a method for approaching comprehension tasks. Psychologists have rarely studied comprehension alone, for comprehension is normally such a private experience that it gives psychologists very little to measure. The usual methodological trick is to embed comprehension itself in other sorts of tasks — tasks which range from simply asking the subject to indicate whether a sentence is true or false to asking him to follow a difficult instruction as fast as possible. In each of these cases, the subject has been tricked into comprehending a sentence, since an understanding of the sentence is required before he can carry out the task. Thus, instead of having to account for comprehension alone, the psychologist has to account for comprehension plus all the subsequent activity that the task requires — e.g. making decisions, responding, crossing out digits, etc. This has led to a formulation of what it is that all these tasks have in common.

The main proposal is that such comprehension tasks can be broken down into four separable stages: (1) a sentence representation stage; (2) another sentence (or picture or knowledge) representation stage; (3) a stage in which the representations of (1) and (2) are compared in some way; and (4) a response stage. These stages help to define what the psychological theory must account for. In particular, it is necessary to know: (a) the form in which sentences are represented at Stages 1 and 2; and (b) the mental operations by which these representations are compared at Stage 3. The present theory therefore makes two strong assumptions. First, the DEEP STRUCTURE ASSUMPTION asserts that a sentence is represented in memory in a form that is equivalent to, or closely related to, its deep underlying linguistic representation. The second assumption, the PRINCIPLE OF CONGRUENCE, used in conjunction with the first, asserts that two such semantic representations are compared for congruence, and in the absence of congruence, there must be mental operations that bring the two representations into congruence.

It is the deep structure assumption and the principle of congruence that lie at the base of the present theory. In the following sections, I will discuss how the deep structure assumption is applied to four different linguistic constructions — the negative, the locative, the comparative, and the active and passive. Armed with this assumption, and the principle of congruence, I will then predict the relative difficulty of each of these constructions as used in a wide variety of comprehension tasks. Then I will review the main results of the experimental literature for each construction and show how the results bear out these predictions, thereby confirming the present theory of comprehension.

2. NEGATION

Negation is undoubtedly one of the most fundamental conceptual devices of language. It is used in the explicit denial of facts (e.g. *Katherine isn't present*), in the affirmation of negatively stated facts (*Katherine is absent*), and so on. From the point of view of syntax, negation is found in vastly different guises — in particles *(not, never, no)*, adjectives *(absent, few)*, adverbs *(hardly, scarcely, seldom)*, verbs *(forget, lack, fail)*, nouns *(absence, lack, failure)*, prepositions *(from, out, off)*, and so on. In short, negation is an extremely heterogeneous phenomenon — even in English. Nevertheless, negation appears to be a phenomenon that should be treated as a single semantic device in language. Indeed, the purpose of section 2 is to present a single unified model of the comprehension of negation — one based on the principles of section 1 — that is capable of accounting for the main facts about all types of negation in the existing psychological literature.

Because negation was one of the first linguistic notions to be studied by psychologists in the last decade, the negation literature is really quite large. The pioneering studies on negation were carried out by Wason (1959, 1961, 1965; Wason and Jones 1963), and this series was followed by investigations by Eifermann (1961), McMahon (1963), Gough (1965, 1966), Slobin (1966), and many others. The main result of these studies can be summarized succinctly: negation is more difficult to comprehend than affirmation. Although this result is hardly surprising, these studies also uncovered a number of other important facts about negation. Unfortunately, the secondary results varied considerably from study to study, so much so that even two apparently similar studies often appear to have quite contradictory results. For example, some studies found that true negative sentences were more difficult to verify than those that were false, whereas other studies found just the opposite. One of the main goals of this section is to reconcile these and other conflicting results on the comprehension of negation.

It was partly because of the inconsistency of the previous results that William Chase and I carried out a series of experiments on an instance of negation that is experimentally much cleaner than any of those studied by previous investigators (Clark and Chase 1972, 1974; Chase and Clark 1971, 1972; Young and Chase 1971; Singer, Chase, Young, and Clark 1971). Indeed, we have found what appears to be the *paradigm case* for the comprehension of negation. I will refer to this case as the 'true' method or model of negation (the meaning of 'true' will become clear later). In addition, Richard Young and William Chase (1971) have shown that negatives can be comprehended by several methods that consist of converting negatives directly into affirmatives and comprehending the resultant affirmatives. I will refer to these methods as the 'conversion' methods or models of negation. One important thing about the 'conversion' models is that they are really just special cases of the 'true' model, although 'conversion' methods produce results that are quite different from those of the 'true' method. The second important thing is that the conflicts in the previous results can be explained by assuming that the subjects in the previous studies were using predominantly one or the other method of negation.

Even more recently, several students and I have carried out a series of studies on other types of negation — in particular, various types of 'implicit' negation, e.g. *absent, few, scarcely any,* and so on. The importance of these studies is that they show that implicit negation is comprehended in the same manner as explicit negation, except for several very important differences, which appear to be closely related to the suppositions of the sentence.

The plan of this section is as follows. In section 2.1, I will present the 'true' and 'conversion' models of negation and their rationale. In that section I will treat only explicit sentence negation, as in the example, *Katherine isn't at home.* In section 2.2, I will review all of the previous literature on this type of negation in order to show that the previous results can be accounted for by the 'true' or 'conversion' models or by some combination of the two. In section 2.3, I will take up the linguistic problem of how to characterize the several different types of negation, especially in terms of supposition; and in section 2.4, I will consider the studies that bear on the psychological properties of those types of negation. In section 2.5, I will consider an instance of 'perceptual' negation, that is, an instance in which a diagram is mentally represented in a negative code that behaves in all other fashions like a linguistic negative. Finally, in section 2.6, I will summarize the main models and findings in negation.

2.1 *The 'True' and 'Conversion' Models of Negation*

The 'true' and 'conversion' models of negation are most easily described within the context of a particular verification task that Chase and I put to our subjects. In it, we presented the subject with a display that contained a sentence on the left and a picture on the right. The subject's task was to read the sentence, then look at the picture, and then press a 'true' or a 'false' button as quickly as possible to indicate whether the sentence was true or false of the picture. The subject was timed from the moment the display appeared to the moment he pushed the button. There were eight possible sentences: *plus is above star, star is above plus, plus is below star, star is below plus, star isn't above plus, plus isn't above star, star isn't below plus,* and *plus isn't below star.* And there were two possible pictures: a star (a typed asterisk) above a plus, and a plus above a star. In all, then, there were 16 displays, four of which contained True Affirmative sentences, four False Affirmative, four True Negative, and four False Negative. The goal we set for ourselves was to account for the variation in the times it took the subjects to decide whether the sentences were true or false.

As proposed in section 1.2, we assumed that the total process could be broken down into four stages. At Stage 1, the subject encodes the sentence in a mental representation of some sort. At Stage 2, he encodes the picture in the same representational format. At Stage 3, the subject compares the representations he has constructed for the sentence and picture to see whether or not they match. And at Stage 4, he takes the output of this comparison stage and converts it into some sort of response. The 'true' and 'conversion' models differ in how the subject is assumed to have represented the sentence at Stage 1; otherwise, the two models are identical.

2.11 The 'true' model of negation

2.111 *The representation problem.* The fundamental question here is, what is the mental representation of a negative sentence? In accordance with the deep structure assumption I am making throughout, the negative sentence is assumed to be represented mentally as something very close to its deep structure. The sentence *A is above B*, for example, is a simple proposition represented, perhaps, in terms of its internal subject-predicate relations as $((A)_{NP}(above\ B)_{VP})_S$. For now, the internal structure of *A is above B* is of little interest, so I will simply represent its deep structure as (*A above B*). But now, when sentence negation is attached to *A is above B*, the result is *A isn't above B*, whose deep structure might look something like the following: $(((A\ above\ B)_S)_{NP}(false)_{VP})_S$. This could be paraphrased as *that A is above B is false* or *it is false that A is above B* or *it isn't the case that A is above B*. For present purposes, I will symbolize the deep structure of this negative simply as (*false* (*A above B*)). It could have been symbolized by a more common notation, say *Neg* (*A above B*), but I prefer the present notation since it makes the semantic nature of the negative explicit. The point of this notation is to show that a negative sentence, like (*false* (*A above B*)), is simply a non-negative proposition embedded in a higher sentence which asserts that that embedded proposition is false. As we will see, there are important consequences that follow from the embedded nature of the negative.

Once this representational scheme has been adopted, the eight basic types of sentences in the verification task can be represented very simply. Consider a schematic picture of an A above a B and the eight possible sentences that could have been paired with that picture. The representations for the eight sentences are shown in the second column of Table I. These eight sentences fall into four categories, True Affirmatives, False Affirmatives, True Negatives, and False Negatives, with a sentence containing *above* and a sentence containing *below* in each category.

The problem of how to represent the pictures at Stage 2 is just as critical as the problem of how to represent the sentences at Stage 1. As discussed in section 1.2, however, the requirement is that the pictures must be represented in the same format as the sentences, and this leaves us with the decision of whether an A above a B is coded as (*A above B*), (*B below A*), (*false* (*B above A*)), or (*false* (*A below B*), all of which are consistent with the picture. Although the experimental evidence cannot be presented here (cf. Clark and Chase 1972, and section 3), it shows that for this particular experiment the picture is coded as (*A above B*) when the sentence contains the word *above*, but as (*B below A*) when the sentence contains the word *below*. These representations are shown in the third column of Table I.

TABLE I. *Sentence representations, picture representations, and latency components for the 'true' model of negation*

Sentence Type	Stage 1 Sentence Representation	Stage 2 Picture Representation	Latency Components
True Affirmative			
	(A above B)	(A above B)	t_0
	(B below A)	(B below A)	$t_0 + a$
False Affirmative			
	(B above A)	(A above B)	$t_0 \quad\ + c$
	(A below B)	(B below A)	$t_0 + a + c$
True Negative			
	(false (B above A))	(A above B)	$t_0 \quad\ + c + (b + d)$
	(false (A below B))	(B below A)	$t_0 + a + c + (b + d)$
False Negative			
	(false (A above B))	(A above B)	$t_0 \qquad\quad + (b + d)$
	(false (B below A))	(B below A)	$t_0 + a \quad\ + (b + d)$

2.112 *The Stage 3 comparison operations.* Stage 3 is meant to decide whether a particular Stage 1 sentence representation (in Table I) is synonymous with its Stage 2 counterpart, the picture representation. Stage 3's job then is to come up with a judgment of 'true' or 'false' about the synonymy of the sentence and picture. For this reason, Stage 3 is said to keep track of a TRUTH INDEX, whose value is *true* or *false*. The goal of Stage 3 is to manipulate the truth index in such a way that the index contains the correct value at the end of the process. It is assumed that the truth index contains the value *true* at the start — that is, the sentence is considered true of the picture until there is evidence to the contrary. Various Stage 3 (mental) operations then change the truth index from *true* to *false*, and even from *false* back to *true* again, depending on the result of various comparisons that the operations carry out.

The heart of the 'true' model of negation is to be found in the mental operations that make up the Stage 3 comparison process. These mental operations could be shown as a flow diagram, as a tree diagram, as a set of branching rules, or otherwise. For convenience, I will represent the mental operations as a set of four branching rules, which are shown in Table II. I will illustrate the use of these rules for the True Negative sentence *B isn't above A,* the fifth line down in Table I. The sentence is represented as *(false (B above A))* at Stage 1; the picture is represented as *(A above B)* at Stage 2. Operation 1 compares the embedded strings *(B above A)* and *(A above B)*, and finds that they do not match. So the process goes to Operation 1a, which changes the presupposed truth value *true* to *false*. Then Opera-

TABLE II. *The comparison process (stage 3) of the 'true' model of negation*

1. Compare the *embedded* strings of sentence and picture.
   A. If they match, go to 2.
   B. If they do not match, go to 1a.
1a. Change value of truth index into its opposite; then go to 2.
2. Compare the *embedding* strings of sentence and picture.
   A. If they match, stop.
   B. If they do not match, go to 2a.
2a. Change value of truth index into its opposite; then stop.

tion 2 compares the embedding strings, *(false* ()) and (()), and finds that they do not match. So the process goes to Operation 2a, which changes the truth index — set at *false* by Operation 1a — from *false* back to *true* again. The final value of the truth index is therefore *true*, which is indeed the correct value for this particular True Negative sentence. Although the four different types of sentences take different paths through these Stage 3 mental operations, careful working through of the four types will convince the reader that the Stage 3 operations of Table II produce the correct answer in every case.

Stage 4 is simply a formal stage in which the outcome of the Stage 3 operations — i.e. the final value of the truth index — is converted into the appropriate response. In Clark and Chase (1972), that response was a push of a button but it could have been the vocalization of the words 'true' or 'false'. In any case, this stage is of little interest here, for the responses are direct and are assumed not to affect the relative verification latencies in the problems we are considering.

2.113 *Predictions of verification latency.* In constructing this model, Chase and I wanted to be able to predict the relative verification latencies for the eight sentence types of Table I. For this purpose, we made several simple assumptions. First, the four stages are carried out in succession. Second, the times taken at each stage are constant from condition to condition. And third, each mental operation at Stage 3 consumes a specific increment of time, and these separate increments are additive. With these assumptions, it is possible to predict the latencies of the eight sentence types of Table I.

At Stage 1, the subject encodes a sentence that contains either *above* or *below*. For reasons that I will discuss in section 3, it was assumed that *below* takes longer to encode at this stage than *above*. To be precise, *below* takes an increment of time a longer to encode. Similarly, it seemed likely a priori that positive and negative sentences would not be encoded in equal times. The assumption was that negatives would take an increment of time b longer to encode than affirmatives. At Stage 3, Operations 1, 1a, 2, and 2a were assumed to consume increments of time x, c, y, and d, respectively. Note that the sentences differ in what Stage 3 operations they require: True Affirmatives require Operations 1 and 2; False Affirmatives require

1, 1a, and 2; True Negatives require 1, 1a, 2, and 2a; and False Negatives require 1, 2, and 2a. All sentences therefore require Operations 1 and 2, and they differ only in whether they require 1a, 2a, or both; that is, they differ in whether they will consume increments of time c, d, or both.

The predictions made by these assumptions about parameters a, b, c, and d are shown for each sentence in Table I. The parameter t_0 is simply a wastebasket category, which contains all the time not taken up by the predicted parameters a, b, c, and d. The True Negative sentence *A isn't below B*, for example, consumes a and b at Stage 1 because it contains *below* and a negative, and it consumes c and d at Stage 3 because it requires both Operations 1a and 2a. Note that b and d are perfectly correlated in this table, making it impossible to separate them out in this experiment. I have therefore listed $(b + d)$ as a single parameter, which I will call simply Negation Time. Similarly, I will call the parameter c Falsification Time. We will need to refer to Negation Time and Falsification Time again and again in our review of the literature.

2.114 *Experimental evidence for the 'true' model.* Data from Clark and Chase (1972) and other related experiments confirm this model with an extraordinary degree of accuracy. In one experiment, twelve subjects were run for 160 trials each in the manner described previously. From the overall data, Below Time a was estimated to be 93 msec, Negation Time $(b + d)$ 685 msec, and Falsification Time c 187 msec. Once these three values were substituted into the formulae of Table I, the latencies predicted by these formulae were very close to the actual overall latencies for these eight types of sentence. Statistically, these three parameters accounted for 99.6% of the variance in the actual latencies. The 'true' model of negation received further support in at least five other experiments; in the latter variants of the initial experiment, the subjects were required to look at the picture first, to attend to particular parts of the picture, or to conform to other differences in procedure. In other words, the 'true' model of negation was supported in a wide variety of conditions, most often accounting for over 97% of the variance in the observed latencies.

So far I have talked of the 'true' model of negation, particularly Stage 3, only in terms of very abstract representations and comparison operations. But all the stages of this model reflect quite accurately what subjects claim they are doing. The typical subject describes his intuitions something like this: 'When I get the sentence *B is above A*, I first look over at the top of the picture.' We presume, for this reason, that he is encoding the picture as (*A above B*), not as (*B below A*). 'But then I notice that the B isn't on top as I expected, so I change my answer to *false* and push the "false" button.' Here we presume that he finds a mismatch at Operation 1 and so must go to Operation 1a, which changes the truth value from *true* to *false,* which then serves as the basis for his button push. 'When I get the sentence *A isn't above B*, again I look at the top of the picture', again presumably encoding the picture as (*A above B*). 'But here I notice that the A *is* above the B, while the sentence says that A is *not* above B. Since this is contradictory, I change my answer to *false*.' Here he has described carrying out Operation 2, finding a mismatch, and then carrying out Operation 2a, which changes the truth value from *true* to *false*. 'With the sentence *B isn't above A*, I look at the top, find that A is above B, and note that the sentence and picture don't match; but I also remember that the sentence is negative so I realize that even though there is a mismatch I must say "true".' Here he is describing finding a mismatch at Operation 1, carrying out Operation 1a, finding a mismatch at Operation 2, and carrying out Operation 2a. In summary, subjects report changing their answer from true to false and back to true again on True Negatives. This is exactly what the model does as well.

In one sense, this model is not particularly new. Wason (1961), for example, formulated an informal model similar to this one based on what his subjects said that they were doing. A similar model of negation was also proposed by Gough (1965) and Slobin (1966). Unfortunately, however, the models they proposed were unable to account for their data in the direct and accurate way that they were able to account for the data in Clark and Chase (1972). The reason, as I will argue below, was because some of the subjects in Wason's and Gough's tasks in particular were treating negatives quite differently from this model. For this reason, Wason and Gough were unable to confirm that the normal process of verifying negative sentences consists of two well-defined operations that consume fixed amounts of time.

2.12   *The 'conversion' methods for comprehending negatives*

The subjects in Clark and Chase (1972) could have used a much more direct method for verifying negative sentences — if they had wanted to. For example, they could have converted the sentence *A isn't above B* immediately into *A is below B* and then looked at the picture for verification. If they had done this consistently for all the negatives, the False Negatives should have been 180 msec slower, rather than 180 msec faster, than the True Negatives, just as the False Affirmatives were 180 msec slower than the True Affirmatives. Evidence internal to the data is therefore in complete agreement with the subjects' reports that they had all used the 'true' method of negation described above.

In principle, however, subjects can make conversions of this sort. Young and Chase (1971) carried out a series of ingenious experiments on the assumption that they could simply instruct subjects to make particular conversions, and if subjects followed these instructions properly, their latencies would change radically from those shown by the subjects in the Clark and Chase experiments. Young and Chase essentially repeated the Clark and Chase experiment just described, but asked their subjects to 'convert' each sentence to another form *before* they looked at the picture. Each subject proceeded through the task using one of four 'conversion' rules: (1) delete the negative and change the preposition, converting e.g. *A isn't above B* into *A is below B*; (2) delete the negative and reverse the two nouns, converting e.g. *A isn't below B* into *B is below A*; (3) changes *below* into *above* and reverse the two nouns, converting e.g. *A isn't below B* into *B isn't above A*; and (4) change *below* into *above* and change positive into negative or vice versa, whichever is appropriate, converting e.g. *A is below B* into *A isn't above B*. Three very reliable subjects worked under each of the four 'conversion' instructions in four different sessions.

Young and Chase predicted that the latencies of their subjects' judgments could be broken down into two parts. First, the conversion itself would take an increment of time k to perform. And second, the 'true' model of negation would work on the semantic representation that results once the 'conversion' had been performed. As illustration, consider the first conversion rule listed above. It changes each negative into an affirmative with the opposite preposition, so that *isn't above* becomes *below* and *isn't below* becomes *above*. Table III shows the sentences as the subjects saw

TABLE III.   *Sentences, sentence representations, and latency components for one 'conversion' method for comprehending negatives*

Sentence Type	Sentence	Stage 1 Sentence Representation	Stage 2 Picture Representation	Latency Components
True Affirmative				
	A is above B	(A above B)	(A above B) t_0	
	B is below A	(B below A)	(B below A) t_0	$+ a$
False Affirmative				
	B is above A	(B above A)	(A above B) t_0	$+ c$
	A is below B	(A below B)	(B below A) t_0	$+ a + c$
True Negative				
	B isn't above A	(B below A)	(B below A) $t_0 + k + a$	
	A isn't below B	(A above B)	(A above B) $t_0 + k$	
False Negative				
	A isn't above B	(A below B)	(B below A) $t_0 + k + a + c$	
	B isn't below A	(B above A)	(A above B) $t_0 + k$	$+ c$

them, the Stage 1 representations of the sentences after conversion, the picture representations, and the appropriate latency components from the 'true' model of negation. Note that the latency components contain k for each negative sentence converted, and no longer contain $(b + d)$, the parameters associated with Negation Time in the 'true' model. In short, the latency components are predicted from a straightforward application of the 'true' model of negation plus Conversion Time k. In the experiments of Young and Chase, this model was supported again with a very high degree of accuracy. With three parameters estimated for each of the three subjects, the model shown in Table III accounted for over 95% of the variance in each of the subjects. Since this kind of accuracy is rare in psychological experiments, these results add considerably to the credibility of this particular 'conversion' model. Young and Chase were just as successful in predicting the latencies under the other three 'conversion' rules.

2.13 *Comparisons of the 'true' and 'conversion' models of negation*

The most important difference between the 'true' and 'conversion' models of negation is that they predict different patterns of latencies for True and False Affirmatives and Negatives. The main comparisons can be seen in Table IV, which lists the predictions of the two models (ignoring the *above-below* difference for the moment). The particular 'conversion' model illustrated here is for rule 1 of the Young and Chase experiment, since that rule is the only one that has been used spontaneously by subjects in other experiments in the literature. First, note that False Affirmatives are predicted to be an increment c slower than True Affirmatives under both models. The reason for this, of course, is that the two models are identical for affirmative sentences. For the negatives, however, True Negatives are c slower than False Negatives under the 'true' model, but c FASTER than False Negatives under the 'conversion' model. To put it another way, there is a true-false by positive-negative interaction under the 'true' model, but no such interaction under the 'conversion' model. The consequence of these effects is that, under the 'true' model, true sentences should be equally as fast overall as false sentences, but under the 'conversion' model true sentences should be an increment c faster overall than false sentences. It is these consequences of the 'true' and 'conversion' models that will allow us to make sense of the previous literature on negation.

TABLE IV.   *The latency components for the 'true' and 'conversion' models of negation*

Sentence Type	'True' Model	'Conversion' Model
True Affirmative	t_0	t_0
False Affirmative	$t_0 + c$	$t_0 + c$
True Negative	$t_0 + c + (b + d)$	$t_0 \qquad + k$
False Negative	$t_0 \qquad + (b + d)$	$t_0 + c + k$

The second important difference between the 'true' and 'conversion' methods is that the 'true' method of negation will work under all circumstances, whereas the 'conversion' method will not. When the subject uses a 'conversion' method, he is normally cheating a bit. By changing *A isn't above B*, for example, into *A is below B*, the subject has lost some of the information in the first sentence, since *below* implies *isn't above*, but *isn't above* does not imply *below*. This particular conversion would result in an incorrect answer for a picture of an A and a B side by side: the sentence *A isn't above* B would be judged true of this picture, while its 'converted' form *A is below B* would incorrectly be judged false. The 'conversion' methods, therefore, can be used correctly only under very special circumstances, as in the Young and Chase experiment in which the subject knew he would never encounter anything but pictures of an A and a B (i.e. a star and a plus) one above the other. It is this fact about the 'conversion' method that justifies the term 'true' in the 'true' method of negation. The 'true' method is the only method that is always applicable and that retains all the information of the negative sentence.

2.2 *Previous Studies of Negation*

These two models of negation — the 'true' and 'conversion' models — can now be profitably applied to the previous research on the comprehension of negative sentences. Although the majority of these studies are verification tasks, they differ in a number of ways. The most immediate difference is in the kinds of evidence that sentences are to be verified against. In some studies, sentences are verified against pictures, as in the Clark and Chase experiments; in others, they are verified against previous knowledge, as in the verification of *Nine isn't an even number*; and in still other cases, they are verified against other sentences, as in *If x precedes y, then y isn't preceded by x*. To be able to form a general theory about the results of these experiments — and the results are indeed very similar — we must assume that all three types of evidence — pictures, previous knowledge, and other sentences — are represented at Stage 2 in the same format. This assumption is a very important one, for without it, we would be forced to formulate a different theory for almost every one of the experiments that follow; with it, the 'true' and 'conversion' models apply accurately to a large number of studies.

The first study to be examined is one of Wason's pioneering studies on negation (Wason 1961) in which subjects were timed as they verified whether sentences like *Nine is not an even number* were true or false. Among his sentences were True Affirmatives (e.g. *Nine is an odd number*), False Affirmatives (*Nine is an even number*), True Negatives (*Nine is not an even number*), and False Negatives (*Nine is not an odd number*). This task is easily formulated in the four-stage model discussed previously. At Stage 1, the subject sets up a representation of the sentence, say *(false (9 is even))*; at Stage 2, he sets up a representation of his a priori knowledge about the number in the sentence, in this case *(9 is odd)*; at Stage 3, he carries out the four-operation comparison process shown in Table II, coming up in this instance with the correct truth value *true*; and at Stage 4, he says 'true'. Thus, if Wason's subjects were actually using the 'true' method of negation, his results should be predicted accurately by the 'true' model.

Wason, however, asked each one of his subjects how he carried out the task. Significantly, he found two types of subjects. The first type — about half the subjects — reported using a method equivalent to the 'true' method of negation.

The second type — the remaining subjects — reported converting *not even* to *odd* and *not odd* to *even* each time they encountered a negative sentence. Since *odd* and *even* are contradictories, this is a perfectly good strategy. (Actually, the use of *not* instead of *n't* probably encouraged this kind of conversion, since it invites contrastive stress — 'Nine is *not* an odd number' — which brings with it the conclusion, 'It is an even one'.) From these reports alone, we should expect the results to show a mixture of the 'true' and 'conversion' models, and this is exactly what Wason found. He found that True Affirmatives took 260 msec less time than False Affirmatives, in agreement with both models. On the other hand, he found True Negatives to be 30 msec faster than False Negatives. The 'true' model predicts that True Negatives should be 260 msec *slower* than False Negatives, whereas the 'conversion' model predicts the opposite. A mixture of the two types of subjects would therefore approximately cancel out the difference between True and False Negatives, just as Wason found. Wason also found that True Negatives elicited the most errors. This would occur because some subjects in the 'true' method would have failed to carry out both Operations 1a and 2a, thus producing the wrong answer; it is only on True Negatives (in the 'true' method) that both comparison operations are required.

In Wason and Jones (1963), a variation of the same experiment was repeated with only slightly different results. Overall, True Affirmatives took 420 msec less than False Affirmatives, but in this case True Negatives were SLOWER than False Negatives by 160 msec. Thus, in this experiment, there must also have been a mix of people using the 'true' and 'conversion' methods, but there should have been slightly more people using the 'true' method. Unfortunately, Wason and Jones did not report on the percentages of subjects using the two methods, although they implied that both kinds of subjects were present. And again, there were more errors on True Negatives than on the other three sentence-types.

Eifermann (1961) repeated the Wason experiment on Hebrew speakers with two types of Hebrew negation. Again, she used sentences like *Seven is not an even number*, in its Hebrew form, and timed subjects' latencies to a correct verification. For the Hebrew negative *lo*, True Affirmatives were verified 67 msec faster than False Affirmatives, and True Negatives 51 msec faster than False Negatives. For the other negative *eyno*, True Affirmatives were 232 msec faster than False Affirmatives, and True Negatives 24 msec slower than False Negatives. Apparently, there was a mixture of people in both groups using the 'true' and 'conversion' methods. In the error data, however, there was a clear tendency in both kinds of negatives for more True Negative errors than False Negative ones. This follows directly from the extra comparison operation required for the True Negative sentences under the 'true' method of negation.

Gough (1965, 1966) used a task in which subjects were first read a sentence and were then shown a picture that was either true or false with respect to the sentence. The sentences affirmed or denied that a boy or a girl hit or kicked a boy or a girl, and the pictures depicted the same possible affirmative events. The subjects were timed from the onset of the picture to their answer. In three separate experiments, Gough found that True Affirmatives were verified faster than False Affirmatives by 125 msec to 165 msec. But in one experiment he found True and False Negatives to have the same latency, in another True Negatives were 55 msec FASTER than False Negatives, and in the final experiment True Negatives were 175 msec SLOWER than False Negatives. That is, the third experiment fits the 'true' method, while the first two do not. However, as Slobin (1966) pointed out, in the first two experiments it was sometimes possible to short-cut the verification of True Negatives merely by noting that the picture was inapplicable to the sentence — e.g. it contained two girls, while the sentence talked only of boys. In the final experiment, however, the sentences and pictures were both restricted to a boy and girl, one hitting the other. In this instance, it is difficult to apply a 'conversion' method or use any shortcuts, but it IS easy to apply the 'true' method, and the latter predicts the data quite well.

Slobin (1966), using a method quite similar conceptually to the third experiment of Gough's, also obtained data that fit the 'true' method quite well. For his subjects, True Affirmatives were 130 msec faster than False Affirmatives, and True Negatives were 230 msec slower than False Negatives. Although these two differences (130 msec and 230 msec) should be the same, they were apparently not reliably different from each other.

An experiment by Trabasso, Rollins, and Shaughnessy (1971) further illustrates the difference between the 'true' and 'conversion' methods of negation, but in quite a different way. Basically, Trabasso et al. attempted to separate out the Stage 1 encoding time for negatives from the Stage 3 comparison times. They were able to do this by presenting a 'sentence' to the subject, who, when he had read and encoded it, pressed a button that presented the verifying picture; Trabasso et al. measured both the encoding time and the verification time. In one experiment, they presented subjects with 'sentences' like *luz green* ('is green') and *kov orange* ('isn't orange') under one of two conditions: in one, the sentences and pictures contained only two colors; in the other, they contained four colors. The subjects in the first condition, then, could use the 'conversion' method, since *kov orange* always implied green and *kov green* always implied orange. And the results showed that the subjects did carry out these conversions. The times at the encoding stage were longer for the negatives (*kov*) than for the affirmatives, since subjects were changing the negatives into the appropriate affirmatives during this preverification phase. But the verification times were approximately the same for affirmatives and negatives. The result is exactly what the 'conversion' method would predict, since at the beginning of the verification stage all the sentences are affirmative and should therefore all take about the same time. The subjects in the second condition, however, because they could not use the 'conversion' method, were forced to use the 'true' method because *kov green* ('not green') did not imply any single color; therefore, *kov green* could not be converted into a single positive color name at the time of encoding. Hence, although the Stage 1 encoding times for negatives were still longer than for affirmatives in this second condition, the Stage 3 verification times for negatives were fully 255 msec longer than for affirmatives, just as the 'true' method would predict.

In another experiment Trabasso et al. presented the picture before the 'sentence'. Here they expected the subjects not to use the 'conversion' method, since the 'true' method in this case would be far simpler to carry out. Indeed, their results fit the predictions of the 'true' method quite well. True Affirmatives were verified 95 msec faster than False Affirmatives, whereas True Negatives were verified 57 msec *slower* than False Negatives, and the difference between 95 msec and 57 msec was not reliable.

In another recent experiment, Wales and Grieve (1969) collected data that further confirm the 'true' method of negation. They asked subjects to verify sentences like *Given 6 and 8, the next number is not 1*, in which the numbers were supposed to add up to 15. Note that in such problems as these, there is no possibility for using a 'conversion' method. As expected, the results are in approximate agreement with the 'true' method. In the group of subjects for whom the difficulty of the addition task was not confounded with verification difficulty, True Affirmatives were verified 140 msec faster than False Affirmatives, and True Negatives 610 msec slower than False Negatives; however, it is not clear whether the difference between 140 and 610 is statistically reliable, and if so, why.

Finally, Greene (1970a, b) asked her subjects to judge whether two sentences were the same or different in meaning. Although this procedure is different from the previous ones, it can be conceptualized in exactly the same way. The process in this case would consist of setting up a mental representation of the first sentence, setting up one of the second sentence, and then comparing the two representations by the 'true' method of negation. Although Greene had her subjects compare the meanings of several kinds of sentences, the conditions of interest here are those in which subjects were given an active sentence, e.g. *x exceeds y*, followed by a negative sentence with the same meaning, *y does not exceed x*, or one with different meaning, *x does not exceed y*. In the present nomenclature the two latter sentences can be considered to be a True Negative and a False Negative, respectively, vis à vis the first sentence. According to her results, subjects were able to verify that a True Negative had the same meaning as the first sentence 730 msec slower than that a False Negative had a different meaning, exactly in agreement with the 'true' method of negation; when there was an additional passive transformation involved (e.g. when the True Negative was *y is not exceeded by x*), then True Negatives were still 280 msec slower than False Negatives. So even in this quite different sort of task, the 'true' method of negation is still able to account for the relative comprehension and comparison times for negative sentences.

In summary, all the studies of explicit negation we have examined are approximately consistent with the 'true' method, the 'conversion' method, or with some combination of the two. I say 'approximately' because there are several results that deviate slightly from the precise predictions of the two models, although these deviations appeared in experiments with considerably more experimental error, with 'looser' timing methods, and so on than the confirming cases. Probably the most precise techniques used were those in the Clark and Chase, Young and Chase, and Trabasso et al. experiments, and they were the studies that showed the most precise confirmation of these models. The 'true' and 'conversion' models therefore find considerable support in the previous literature. This is not to say that these two models explain everything. For one thing, previous studies show considerable variation in the relative difficulty of negative sentences. In Trabasso et al., for example, negatives were approximately 200 msec slower than affirmatives, while in the Clark and Chase experiment, negatives were 685 msec slower than affirmatives. Why should Negation Time vary so much between these two studies? Part of the answer, I will argue, is to be found in differences in the scope of negation. But to discuss this point and the other studies on negation, I must first describe, classify, and represent the different types of negation found in English.

2.3 Types of Negation in English

As I pointed out earlier, English contains many types of negation other than the simple sentence negation. Negation, for example, seems to be implicit in many single lexical items, like *absent, forget, few, small, below,* and so on. What are the differences between these various types of negation? One important distinction to be made is between explicit and implicit negation, between e.g. *isn't present* and *absent*. Although this division can be made on syntactic grounds, the division will also be shown to be the result of differing presuppositions on the part of the speaker. A second important distinction to be made is between full and quantifier negation, between e.g. *not many* and *few*. Although there are probably many other possible distinctions among negatives, these two are important because they can be shown to be implicated directly in the way negatives are comprehended.

2.31 Explicit versus implicit negation

The sentence *Helen isn't home* denies that Helen is at home. When would it be appropriate for me to make such a denial? If I thought that you had expected Helen to be home, or had said so, or had implied so in what you had just said, I would be very likely to say, *Helen isn't at home*. Note that it seems appropriate to say *I know you think Helen is at home, but she isn't at home,* but quite inappropriate to say *I know you think Helen is at school, but she isn't at home*. These examples hint at the fact that a speaker usually makes an assumption about the beliefs (or apparent beliefs) of his listener whenever he utters a denial. Specifically, he normally supposes that the listener does or could well believe in the truth of what is being denied. In saying *Helen isn't at home,* the speaker supposes, for any one of a number of reasons, that the listener believes that Helen is or might be at home. As Wason (1965) pointed out, *The whale isn't a fish* is a plausible negative since it is reasonable to assume that a listener might think that whales are fish; but *The whale isn't a bird,* though true, sounds highly incongruous, for surely no one could believe that a whale is a bird. It appears, then, that a full representation of what a listener understands of a negative sentence ought to contain something about the sentence's (or speaker's) suppositions.

Denials of this sort, however, appear to be different from other types of negatives, and this distinction coincides with Klima's (1964) distinction between affirmative and negative sentences. Negatives can be identified, according to Klima, by whether they can co-occur with *any* in the same clause and with *either* as a final tag when the negative is in the second of two *and*-conjoined clauses. Consider the criterion of *any*-acceptance first. *None* is negative since **4d** is acceptable:

4 a) All of the men had some dinner.
 b) *None of the men had some dinner.
 c) *All of the men had any dinner.
 d) None of the men had any dinner.

The criterion of *either*-conjunction leads to the same conclusion, since **5d** is also acceptable:

5 a) The men left and all of the women left too.
 b) *The men stayed and none of the women left too.
 c) *The men left and all of the women left either.
 d) The men stayed and none of the women left either.

By these two criteria, there are a number of specific words in English that turn out to be negative, e.g. *scarcely, hardly, few, seldom, little,* etc., besides the obvious ones, e.g. *not, no, none, never,* etc.

The interesting point about these criteria is that they fail to identify such words as *absent, forget, except,* and *without* as negative, even though these words are approximately synonymous with expressions that are considered negative, i.e. *not present, not remember, but not,* and *not with* respectively. Thus, Klima's criteria can be used to separate out explicit negatives (like *not present*) from implicit negatives (like *absent*): the explicit negatives conform to his co-occurrence rules, whereas the implicit negatives fail to do so. A quick perusal of English reveals any number of explicit/implicit pairs: *not have/lack, not succeed/fail, not successful/unsuccessful,* and so on.

The explicit/implicit distinction can be seen most clearly in a striking minimal pair — *few* (an explicit negative) and *a few* (an implicit negative). They are distinguished by *any*-acceptance:

6 a) Few of the men ate any dinner.
 b) *A few of the men ate any dinner.

and by *either*-conjunction:

    7 a) Many men stayed and few women left either.

      b) *Many men stayed and a few women left either.

Although at first glance *few* and *a few* appear to mean the same thing, a closer look shows that they differ in what they suppose of the listener's or speaker's expectations. The sentence *Few men left*, for example, supposes that many or all of the men were expected to leave. Thus, of the two sentences,

    8 a) I expected all the men to leave, but few did.

      b) *I expected none of the men to leave, but few did.

only **8a** contains an acceptable prior expectation. On the other hand, *A few men left* supposes that few or perhaps none of the men were expected to leave. Thus *a few* has exactly the opposite effects on acceptability as *few*, as can be seen in **9**:

    9 a) *I expected all of the men to leave, but a few men did.

      b) I expected none of the men to leave, but a few men did.

Note that **9a** can be made acceptable by adding *only* before *a few*, since *only* is an explicit negative that thereby makes the sentence acceptable (cf. Horn 1969); **9a** can also be made acceptable by placing contrastive stress on *few*, which has approximately the same consequence as adding *only*.

    In short, explicit negatives actually deny positive suppositions on the part of the speaker or listener (*No, it isn't true. Few men left.*), while implicit negatives merely affirm the already negative suppositions of the speaker or listener (*Yes, it's true. A few men left.*). In this sense, the explicit negatives really do deny, while the implicit negatives actually affirm.

    The main problem is how to represent these subtle differences in the notation for their semantic representation. The differences between **10a**, **11a**, and **12a** seem to be appropriately captured in the representations of **10b**, **11b**, and **12b**, respectively, whose paraphrases are shown in **c** in each case:

    10 a) Many men aren't leaving.

       b) (false (suppose (men (men are many) leave)))

       c) It is false to suppose that many men are leaving.

    11 a) Few men are leaving.

       b) (men (false (suppose (men are many))) leave)

       c) It is false to suppose that the men who are leaving are many.

    12 a) A few men are leaving.

       b) (men (suppose (false (men are many))) leave)

       c) It is correct to suppose that the men who are leaving are not many.

The main point of this notation is to show how these three types of negation differ in their scope. In **10**, the whole sentence is found within the scope of the *false*; in **11**, it is the supposition that is denied; and in **12**, *false* lies within the scope of the supposition. To put it still another way, *Few men are leaving* makes the assumption that some men are leaving, but asserts that the number is not many, whereas *A few men are leaving* makes the assumption that the number of men referred to is not many and it affirms that this number is leaving.

We now have come to the point where we can distinguish three different 'dimensions': positive-negative, affirmation-denial, and agreement-contradiction. First of all, a sentence with a negative is not necessarily a denial. A denial is specifically a sentence that asserts that something is false, where that something is presupposed to be possible. Some negatives are not denials, e.g. *A few men left*, since it is only their suppositions that are negative. It is clear under these distinctions, then, that Klima's criterion of *either*-conjunction is a criterion for denials, not for negation. Note **13** and **14**:

13 The men without hats caught cold, and the women who didn't wear hats caught cold
   a) too.
   b) *either.

14 The men who caught cold were without hats, and the women who caught cold didn't wear hats
   a) *too.
   b) either.

In **13**, there is clearly a negative *(didn't)* within the second main clause, but the second clause itself is an affirmation, so it takes *too*, not *either*. On the other hand, the second main clause of **14** is a denial, so it takes *either*, not *too*. The negative in **13**, since it is contained in a restrictive relative clause, is part of a presupposition of the second clause: the second clause of **13** presupposes that there were women who didn't wear hats (cf. Vendler 1967). If we think of a sentence as consisting of an assertion plus perhaps some presuppositions, then a negative in the assertion makes the sentence a denial, whereas a negative in the presupposition leaves the sentence simply as an affirmation. Notice that this is just the difference I have tried to capture between *few*, a denial with a positive supposition, and *a few*, an affirmation with a negative supposition. Finally, agreement-contradiction is distinguishable from both positive-negative and affirmation-denial. An agreement can be either positive or negative, and either an affirmation or a denial:

15 a) So Mary has been here all day? Indeed, she has.
   b) So Mary hasn't been here all day? Indeed, she hasn't.

And so can a contradiction:

16 a) So Mary has been here all day? I'm sorry, she hasn't.
   b) So Mary hasn't been here all day? I'm sorry, she has.

The matter is certainly more complicated than I have indicated here, but these are the main distinctions to be made.

Another example of a minimal pair is *not present* (an explicit negative) and *absent* (an implicit one). To say *John isn't present* and *John is absent* is clearly to refer to the same objective situation. Again, the difference between them lies in whether one wants to deny the supposition that John is present, as in *John isn't present*, or to affirm the supposition that John isn't present as in *John is absent*.

I should add one caution here. I have pointed out that the supposition of the sentence normally refers to assumptions that the speaker has supposed that the listener has made about the subject at hand. However, this does not appear to be a hard and fast rule. When I say *Helen isn't at home,* what it appears that I am saying is really this: 'Suppose that Helen is at home; well, that supposition is false.' The supposition is like a temporary condition set up so that I can make some point with reference to that condition. The temporary condition set up, of course, will not be an arbitrary one; it will normally be pertinent to the speaker's and listener's beliefs at the moment. Furthermore, it appears that what I have been calling supposition is closely related, if not identical, to presupposition, as identified e.g. by Fillmore (1970) or Lakoff (1970). A presupposition of a sentence is a proposition that must be true for the sentence to be 'felicitous'. For example, for John to say, 'You should stop beating your wife', he would have to believe that you have been beating your wife; otherwise, the sentence would be infelicitous. The sentence *I know you have never beaten your wife, but you should stop beating her* is infelicitous (and unacceptable). This type of unacceptability seems to have its parallel in negation; e.g. *I know you think that John is absent, and he isn't present.* The unacceptability is not quite as severe here possibly, but it seems to be similar in origin. On the other hand, the usual test for whether a part of the meaning of a sentence is a presupposition or not is whether that part changes meaning under negation. For example, *Stop beating your wife* and *Don't stop beating your wife* both presuppose that you have been beating your wife, so the latter is a presupposition, not an implication of the first two sentences. In the same sense, it seems that both *John is absent* and *John isn't absent* 'presuppose' an assumption (perhaps very temporary) that John isn't present. But it is impossible to apply the same criterion to *John isn't present,* which already contains an explicit sentence negative. I have, therefore, tentatively called the phenomenon just discussed for negatives 'supposition', instead of 'presupposition', but the hypothesis is that supposition and presupposition are probably very closely related. For now, we can consider supposition to be simply a temporary condition or assumption set up for the sentence.

2.32 *Full versus quantifier negation*

The second distinction to be made among the negatives is between full and quantifier negatives. The distinction is parallel to the difference between antonyms that are contradictories and those that are contraries (cf. Lyons 1968). *Present* and *absent* are contradictories, since *not present* implies *absent* and vice versa. In contrast, *many* and *few* are only contraries, since *not many* does not necessarily imply *few,* although *few* always implies *not many.* To put this another way, *present* and *absent* are contradictories since *John is neither present nor absent* is a contradictory sentence; *many* and *few* are contraries since *There were neither many nor few people at the movie* is not contradictory. Thus, I wish to call *absent* a full negative, and *few* a quantifier negative.

This distinction is quite independent of the explicit-implicit distinction. Therefore, there are four possible classes of negatives: (1) explicit full negatives, like *not present*; (2) implicit full negatives, like *absent*; (3) explicit quantifier negatives, like *few*; and (4) implicit quantifier negatives, like *a few*. Unfortunately, this brings up a notational problem. The notation I have used for *few* is indistinguishable from the one that would be used for *not many*. The *false* applied to *many* to produce *few* is actually only applied to a feature — the feature +Polar — of the word *many*; in contrast, the *false* applied to *many* to get *not many* applies somehow to the whole lexical item. It is not immediately obvious how this difference is easily represented in a simple notation, so I have ignored this problem in the present section. The convention to be used here is that a *false* applied to a quantifier produces a quantifier negative only (e.g. *few*), and not a full negative (e.g. *not many*). Ignoring the difference between the two types of *false* has no consequences in the present chapter.

By this characterization, full and quantifier negatives differ slightly in scope. A full negative will always contain complete propositions or lexical items within its scope, as in e.g. *not many*. In contrast, a quantifier negative will contain only a single feature such as +Polar within its scope, as in e.g. *few*. This difference in scope will be important in a review of the studies that compare different types of negation.

2.4 *Previous Studies of Implicit Negation*

Although there are few studies of implicit negation in the literature, the studies that exist show that the 'true' method of negation is just as applicable to implicit negation as to explicit negation, although with several important differences. These studies also suggest a second hypothesis, something I will call the scope of the negation hypothesis, which is this: the greater the scope of the negative the more difficult the negative is to comprehend. More specifically, this hypothesis asserts that Negation Time will increase for increases in scope of negation. In order to examine these two hypotheses, I will review three series of experiments, one on *except*, a second on *not present* and *absent*, and a third on a number of explicitly or implicitly negative quantifiers. Next, I will collect together all the Negation and Falsification Times found in the literature and compare them in the light of these two hypotheses. Finally, I will discuss two previous studies and how the notions of supposition just discussed apply to them.

2.41 *Except*

The first implicit negative to be examined is *except*. It has been carefully investigated by Sheila Jones (1966a, b; 1968) in an important series of experiments on the use of *except* in instructions. These experiments are particularly significant, because they show that the 'true' method of negation is applicable to instructions as well as verification tasks and to implicit as well as explicit negatives, and because they give the first evidence for the scope of negation hypothesis.

In her experiments, Jones gave her subjects a pencil, a sheet of paper filled with the digits 1 through 8 in a random order, and asked them to cross out certain digits according to instruction. She timed them for each sheet of digits they crossed out. Some subjects were given the 'inclusive' instructions: 'Mark the numbers 3, 4, 7, and 8', and others were given the 'exclusive' instructions: 'Mark all numbers except 1, 2, 5, and 6.' It should be noted that the two instructions are equivalent in two important respects. Both require the subject to keep only four digits in mind, and both require him to mark out digits 3, 4, 7, and 8. The important difference is that the inclusive instruction is positive, and the exclusive instruction implicitly negative.

Before examining the results, however, we should attempt to formulate how Jones' subjects presumably would have represented the instructions mentally. The inclusive instruction **17a** might best be represented as a conditional, as in **17b**, which is paraphrased in **17c**:

17 a) Mark the numbers 3, 4, 7, 8.
b) (you mark X (if (X is (3 or 4 or 7 or 8))))
c) Mark X (the number you are currently checking) if X is 3, 4, 7, or 8.

The corresponding exclusive instruction, its representation, and its paraphrase are given in **18**:

18 a) Mark all numbers except 1, 2, 5, 6.
b) (you mark X (if (false (X is (1 or 2 or 5 or 6)))))
c) Mark X if it isn't true that X is 1, 2, 5, or 6.

That is, these two instructions are identical in form, except that the inclusive instruction contains a positive conditional where the exclusive one contains a negative one. Both instructions can be thought of as consisting of two parts: a *test* plus a *command*. The test (if . . .) is positive for the inclusive instruction and negative for the exclusive instruction, whereas the command (Mark X) is positive under both instructions.

The effects of these instructions on crossing-out time are now easy to predict, since each test (of each test-plus-command instruction) can be viewed simply as a specific instance of the 'true' method of negation described earlier. At stage 1 of that method, the subject codes the test as, for example, (*false* (X is (1 or 2 or 5 or 6))); at Stage 2, he codes the number he is currently testing, say (X is 2); at Stage 3, he compares the two codes by the four-operation comparison process shown in Table II; and at Stage 4, he enters the answer into the command and carries out the command. By this analysis, the inclusive instructions contain a test that is a True Affirmative half the time and a False Affirmative the other half of the time. In contrast, the exclusive instructions contain a test that is a True Negative half the time and a False Negative the other half of the time. Since affirmatives require one less Stage 3 comparison operation, overall, than negatives, the inclusive instructions should be faster than the exclusive instructions, even though both instructions make the subject carry out an equal number of tests and exactly the same commands. In agreement with this prediction, Jones found that the inclusive instructions took about 67% as much time as the exclusive ones.

Jones (1966a) also carried out an interesting variation of the above instructions. Instead of using the inclusive and exclusive instructions equivalent in their test sets, she changed the inclusive instruction to read 'Mark the numbers 1, 3, 4, 6, 7' and the exclusive instruction to read 'Mark all numbers except 2, 5, 8'. For this inclusive instruction 5/8 of the tests will be True Affirmative, 3/8 will be False Affirmative, but each test will take longer than before, since each X must be tested against five, instead of four, members of the test set. For the exclusive instruction, 5/8 of the tests will be the more difficult True Negative, and 3/8 will be False Negative, but here each negative test will take less time than before since the test set consists of three, instead of four, digits. Jones found that under these instructions the difference between the two instructions was considerably reduced: the inclusive instructions were carried out in about 95% of the time it took for the exclusive instructions, although the difference was still statistically significant. This agrees with intuition that the more digits there are to be marked out, the easier it will be to follow the exclusive instructions. If the set of digits to be marked out includes as many as seven of the eight digits, the exclusive instructions, which specify the single digit *not* to be marked out, should be easier to follow than the inclusive instructions, which specify the seven digits that are to be marked out, just because the negative test set is so much smaller than the positive test set.

The errors subjects made in Jones' experiments demonstrate another phenomenon, but it appears to be independent of the 'true' model of negation. On the inclusive instructions in the second experiment of Jones (1966a), she found fewer 'false positive' errors (instances of digits incorrectly marked out) than 'omissions' (failures to mark out a digit that should have been marked out); the error percentages were 2% and 6%, respectively. In contrast, the exclusive instructions showed more 'false positive' errors than 'omissions', 8% to 4%. The same pattern of errors is found in Jones 1966b, with the four conditions eliciting 1%, 6%, 8% and 6% errors, respectively. Such a pattern can be accounted for under the assumption that people are more apt to miss a digit they are looking for than select a digit as being in the test set when it is not. This could well be a perceptually motivated phenomenon based on the way people search the visual features of a digit for a match with the digits in memory. In any case, the pattern could not have been produced by the 'true' model, since for the inclusive instructions it would predict more False Affirmative errors ('false positive' errors) than True Affirmative errors ('omissions') and for the exclusive instructions more True Negative errors ('omissions') than False Negative errors ('false positive' errors). The data were just the reverse in both cases. In agreement with the 'true' model, however, there were more errors on the negative than affirmative instructions in all the experiments. This effect is independent of the possible perceptual scanning strategies.

In another experiment, Jones (1968) gave her subjects either explicit or implicit negations as instructions for the same type of task. Her instructions were the following:

19 a) 'Mark all the numbers except 2, 5, 8'
   b) 'Except for the numbers 2, 5, 8, mark all the rest'
20 a) 'Mark all the numbers, but not 2, 5, 8'
   b) 'Do not mark the numbers 2, 5, 8; mark all the rest'

The instructions in **19** contain the implicit negative *except*, whereas those in **20** contain the explicit negative *not*. Her main finding was that the implicit instructions **19** were easier to carry out than the explicit ones **20**. She also found that when she asked her subjects what they were doing both just before and just after the task, they overwhelmingly tended to restate the instruction they were given as an *implicit* negative 'self-instruction', especially as instruction **19a**.

If the theory of comprehension we are examining is valid for this task, we must be able to trace the difference between the implicit and explicit instructions to a difference in the mental representations. At first glance, the two instructions appear to be identical: they both specify only the set that is not to be marked. But on closer examination, they differ in one important respect. If we again think of each instruction as consisting of a test plus a command, the explicit negative instructions place the negative on the command and test together, whereas the implicit negative instructions place the negative on only the test, as we saw above. The representation for **19** and for **20** would therefore look something like **19c** and **20c**, respectively:

19 c) (you mark X (if (false (X is (2 or 5 or 8)))))
20 c) (false (you mark X (if (X is (2 or 5 or 8)))))

So in the explicit instruction **20**, the test itself will be either a True or False Affirmative, but the command — the consequent — will be either a True or False Negative; the reverse holds for the implicit instruction **19**. That **19** was easier to carry out than **20** is therefore reflected in a real difference in their mental representations.

Here is the first evidence we have that scope of negation is important. Note that the scope of negation in the easier instruction **19** is less than in **20**, where the negation includes everything in its scope. The difficulty in handling the wider negative scope of **20** would also explain why Jones' subjects preferred to reformulate it as the referentially equivalent, but psychologically easier, implicit instruction **19**.

2.42 *Present and absent*

The next implicit negative to be examined is *absent*, a full negative like *except*. *Absent* cannot take *any* (**John has been absent at any parties this month*), whereas its explicit negative counterpart *not present* can (*John hasn't been present at any parties this month*). *Absent* also does not allow *either*-conjunction (*John was *gone and Mary was absent either*), although *not present* does (*John was gone and Mary wasn't present either*). The most important property of *absent*, however, is that it is referentially identical with *not present*: the sentences *John is absent* and *John isn't present* will clearly always describe the same referential situation. The difference between them, as I pointed out before, is in their suppositions. *John isn't present* denies the supposition that John is present, whereas *John is absent* affirms a supposition that John isn't present. Concomitant with this difference in supposition is a difference in scope of negation: the scope of the negative in *isn't present* is larger than the scope of the negative in *absent*. So here again we have a case in which we can see whether the 'true' method of negation applies to implicit negatives as well as whether the scope of negation hypothesis is confirmed or not. The relevant experiments are reported in Clark and Young (in preparation).

The predictions of the 'true' method of negation are more clearly visible after the assumed mental representations of the possible sentences have been made explicit. The four types of sentences used in Clark and Young are shown in **21** through **24** followed by their representations and the approximate paraphrases of those representations:

21 a) A is present.
  b) (true (suppose (A is present)))
  c) It is correct to suppose that A is present.
22 a) A isn't present.
  b) (false (suppose (A is present)))
  c) It is false to suppose that A is present.
23 a) A is absent.
  b) (true (suppose (false (A is present))))
  c) It is correct to suppose that it is false that A is present.
24 a) A isn't absent.
  b) (false (suppose (false (A is present))))
  c) It is false to suppose that it is false that A is present.

The *not present* versus *absent* difference is now well defined, since *A isn't present* and *A is absent* have a *true* and a *false* interchanged: 'It is *false* to suppose that it is *true* that A is present' versus 'It is *true* to suppose that it is *false* that A is present'. In the actual task of Clark and Young (in preparation), subjects were asked to verify a sentence describing whether a star or plus was or wasn't present or absent; on the opposite side of the display, the picture was always either a star (*) or a plus (+). The subjects were timed from the moment they looked at the display to the moment they pushed the 'true' or 'false' button.

The 'true' model must be recast slightly for *present* and *absent*, since the model must now be able to accommodate the *suppose* of the sentence representations and the double negative in *isn't absent*. At Stage 1, the subject would represent the sentences as in **21** through **24**. At Stage 2, he would represent the pictures either as (*star is present*) or (*plus is present*), depending on which figure was there. It is at Stage 3 that a problem arises, since the four-operation process (in Table II) has no devices for handling either *suppose* or double negatives. The solution I will use temporarily is simply to ignore the embedding strings labeled *suppose* and to add a third pair of operations (Operations 3 and 3a), which compare the next embedding strings out and change the truth index on finding a mismatch. The result of this proposal is that the 'true' model applies to *not present* and *absent* in the identical way and that the false double negative *isn't absent* should be slowest to verify since its truth index would have to be changed four times.

The results of Clark and Young confirm the predictions from the 'true' model of negation. True *present* statements were verified about 180 msec faster than false *present* statements, just as they should be for affirmative sentences. In contrast, both true *not present* and true *absent* statements were verified 95 msec slower, respectively, than their false counterparts, just as they should be for negative sentences. The two increments of time here should be the same if subjects were always going through the processes exactly as outlined above; the difference between the two increments, however, suggests that some subjects might have been using a method to be described in 2.5 below. Finally, true *isn't absent* statements were verified more quickly than false ones; however, almost all the subjects reported 'converting' *isn't absent* into *is present*, making the predictions for the *isn't absent* case inapplicable.

These results also support the scope of negation hypothesis. It was found that *absent* statements were 371 msec slower, overall, than *present* statements, whereas *not present* statements were fully 640 msec slower than *present* statements. That is, *isn't present* took 270 msec longer than *absent* to verify. This difference cannot be accounted for by differences in the referential properties of *isn't present* and *absent*, since there are none. It also cannot be accounted for by the extra reading time of *isn't present* over *absent*, since careful measurements show that reading could account for no more than 20 msec of this difference and it probably accounts for less. The sole difference between *isn't present* and *absent* is therefore in the semantic representations of these two expressions: the negative of *isn't present* contains the supposition, while the negative of *is absent* is contained in the supposition. The 270 msec difference — at least most of it — must therefore be associated with this difference in representation.

What is the source of the 270 msec difference? There are two possibilities. (1) *Isn't present* could take longer to represent at Stage 1 than *absent*. Or (2) *isn't present* could consume more time in the Stage 3 operations than *absent*. Although very little evidence is available on this issue, one of Jones' results already discussed seems to suggest that (2) might be true. She found that *except* instructions were easier than *but not* instructions, and we noted that this difference was related to a difference in scope of negation in the representations of these instructions. The important point, though, is that her subjects presumably comprehended the instruction just once — at the beginning of the task — but used the instruction over and over again in crossing out the digits. In other words, Stage 1 occurred once, but Stage 3 recurred throughout the experiment. The advantage of *except* over *but not* must therefore be located at Stage 3. This suggests that the *d* increment, the time taken by Operation 2a in the comparison process of Table II, is simply longer when the *false* dominates more in its embedded string, as it does for both *isn't present* (vs. *absent*) and *but not* (vs. *except*).

Obviously, the evidence available does not allow us to specify the mechanisms that underlie the scope of negation hypothesis. We must be satisfied here with a statement of the hypothesis; we will have to account for it later. The actual mechanism might necessitate a slight change in the specific form of the Stage 3 operations listed in Table II, but the operations must nevertheless be approximately correct, since they are necessary to account for the explicit negatives, for *isn't present, absent, except*, and *but not*, and for several other examples that follow. It is probably just as important as the hypothesis itself that we have identified an important difference in comprehension that can only be specified as a difference in semantic representations of sentences; in particular, the semantic difference is in the form of the suppositions of the sentences. We will now examine another instance where supposition is critical in accounting for the comprehension of certain implicit negatives.

2.43 *The Just and Carpenter study*

Marcel Just and Patricia Carpenter (1971) have completed a comparative study of several types of negation in English. In their task, they asked subjects to verify sentences like *Most of the dots are black* and *A small proportion of the dots are black* against pictures that contained either 14 black dots and 2 red dots or the reverse. Just and Carpenter explicitly set out to investigate three categories of negation. In Category 1, there were three exemplars of explicit negation: (A) *The dots are red* vs. *The dots aren't red*; (B) *There are red dots* vs. *There are no red dots*; and (C) *All of the dots are red* vs. *None of the dots are red*. (Unlike the pictures for Categories 2 and 3, the pictures paired with the Category 1 sentences contained either all red or all black dots.) Clearly, Exemplar A contains a sentence negation, while in Exemplars B and C, the negative encompasses only the quantifier and therefore has a slightly smaller scope. Category 2 contained exemplars of explicit quantifier negation: (D) *Most of the dots are red* vs. *Hardly any of the dots are red;* (E) *Lots of the dots are red* vs. *Scarcely any of the dots are red;* and (F) *Many of the dots are red* vs. *Few of the dots are red*. Finally, Category 3 contained three exemplars of implicit quantifier negation: (G) *The majority of the dots are red* vs. *The minority of the dots are red;* (H) *A large proportion of the dots are red* vs. *A small proportion of the dots are red;* and (I) *14 out of 16 dots are red* vs. *2 out of 16 dots are red*.

The results of the Just and Carpenter study support the 'true' model of negation in several very important ways. First, they found that negatives were more difficult than affirmatives in all three categories. Second, they found that in Categories 1 and 2, which contained all explicit negatives, True Positives were faster than False Positives, and True Negatives were slower than False Negatives. For Category 1 this is a replication of previous results, but for Category 2 this is a result that shows that the 'true' model of negation also holds for explicitly negative quantifiers, like *few, scarcely any*, and *hardly any*. But third, they found, quite unexpectedly, that in Category 3 True Positives and True Negatives were both verified faster than their false counterparts. Although this result appeared somewhat mysterious at first, Just and Carpenter showed that this apparent inconsistency was nonetheless in agreement with the 'true' model of negation.

Just and Carpenter accounted for the Category 3 inconsistency by the way the pictures were coded for those exemplars. (I have recast Just and Carpenter's explanation in terms of supposition to make it compatible with the present analysis of negatives.) Consider *many-few* (a Category 2 pair of quantifiers) vs. *many-a few* (substituting for a Category 3 pair of quantifiers). When verifying the true sentence *Many of the dots are black* — i.e. (*true* (*suppose* (*dots* (*dots black*) *are many*))) —, the subject can choose whether to code the majority of the dots in the picture (the 14 black), or the minority (the 2 red). In the former case, he would code the picture as (*dots* (*dots black*) *are many*), but in the latter case, he would code it as (*false* (*dots* (*dots red*) *are many*)). Note that the coding for the majority of the dots will be congruent with the sentence, but the coding of the minority will not. Just and Carpenter assumed that subjects coded the majority of dots for both *many* and *few* (Category 2); this would produce the correct predictions from the 'true' model of negation. In contrast, they were assumed to code the majority and minority, respectively, for *many* and *a few* (Category 3); this likewise allows the correct predictions from the 'true' model. Restated slightly, subjects were always assumed to code the picture in terms of the supposition of the sentence: *many* and *few* both contain suppositions about the majority of the dots; but *many* and *a few* contain suppositions about the majority and minority of the dots, respectively. This coding is natural for other reasons. *Many* and *few* respectively affirm and deny something about the majority of the dots; in contrast, *many* and *a few* are both affirmations, one about the majority of the dots and the other about the minority.

In order to justify this explanation of the difference between Categories 2 and 3, Just and Carpenter re-ran the two categories, but this time they presented the pictures a half-second *before* the sentence appeared. In this way the coding of the pictures could not be contingent on the type of negative in the sentence. In one condition, the subjects were instructed to code the majority of the dots from the picture, and in the other, the minority. Their results here were in full agreement with their previous explanation. When subjects coded the majority of the dots only, Categories 2 and 3 were in complete agreement, in contrast with the results of the first experiment. And when subjects coded the minority only, the two categories were again in complete agreement, but in this case True Positives and False Negatives were slower, instead of faster, than False Positives and True Negatives, respectively. This result is also consistent with the 'true' model of negation, once the codings of the pictures produced by the new instructions have been taken into account. The conclusion is that when subjects are forced to code the pictures in one particular way, the subjects then verify the exemplars of Categories 2 and 3 in exactly the same way. In all, the Just and Carpenter results fit nicely into the present unified explanation for negation.

The Just and Carpenter results also support the scope of negation hypothesis. Their exemplars of negation can be approximately ordered for decreasing scope. Exemplar A is sentence negation and should have roughly the greatest scope; Exemplars B and C have less scope than A since they negate only a quantification; Exemplars D, E, and F are all explicit quantifier negatives, so they are next; Exemplars G, H, and I have the least scope, since their negatives are included within the supposition. Significantly, the Negation Time of these four groups of exemplars decreased approximately with scope (cf. below). This evidence, however, is not as direct as in the *present-absent* and *except* examples above, since so many other things seem to be varying at the same time in Just and Carpenter's exemplars.

2.44 *Other studies of implicit negation*

Scattered throughout the psychological literature are a number of studies that show that certain other negative adjectives and prepositions have properties consonant with the 'true' model of negation. Although I report on these studies in more detail in sections 3 and 4, I will summarize that evidence briefly here.

In Clark (1969a) I reviewed the previous literature on deductive reasoning that used problems of the sort, 'If John is better than Pete, and Dick is better than John, then who is best?' In problems such as this, the comparative adjective could be either a positive adjective or an implicit negative one — e.g. *better* or *worse*. The previous literature on these problems shows that the positive adjectives in comparative form are easier to comprehend than the negative adjectives. Problems with the comparatives of *good, much, fast, far, tall, happy, warm, deep, old*, and *high* were solved consistently faster or with fewer errors than problems with their respective implicitly negative opposites. This evidence, along with the results of Just and Carpenter, leads to the tentative conclusion that all the lexically marked adjectives like *bad, little, slow*, etc., are implicit (quantifier) negatives.

Prepositions can also be either implicit full negatives or implicit quantifier negatives. *Out*, for example, is a full negative preposition, since *John isn't in the room* and *John is out of the room* imply each other. The three pairs of full negative prepositions in English are *to* and *from*, *in* and *out*, and *on* and *off*. Carole Offir and I recently studied *to* and *from* and *into* and *out of* in a verification task and found that sentences with *to* and *into* were verified more quickly than sentences with *from* and *out of*, respectively. Examples of preposition pairs that contain implicit quantifier negatives are *above* and *below*, *ahead of* and *behind*, and *in front of* and *in back of*.

They are quantifier pairs since, for example, *A isn't above B* does not imply *A is below B* although the latter implies the former. Among pairs of this sort, a review of the literature shows that *above, on top of, in front of, ahead of*, and *before* (the positive members of the pairs) are comprehended more quickly than their negative opposites *below, under, in back of, behind*, and *after*.

In summary, the evidence for the comprehension of certain implicitly negative adjectives and prepositions is in general agreement with the 'true' model of negation.

2.45 *Comparison of previous studies on negation*

It is instructive at this point to collect together the results from a number of past studies, for this evidence adds somewhat more support to the scope of negation hypothesis as well as to the 'true' model of negation. In Tables V through VIII, I have listed the Negation and Falsification Times from the studies that have measured the latencies in the verification of positive and negative sentences from the moment the sentence was presented to the moment the subject responded. In each table, I have listed the investigators of the particular negative, the negative studied (the positive counterpart of which is usually obvious), and the Negation and Falsification Times for each negative. The four tables list, respectively, explicit full negatives, explicit quantifier negatives (with two exceptions to be noted later), implicit full negatives, and implicit quantifier negatives. The Falsification Times were estimated in each case from the difference between false and true positive sentences only, since in many studies the subjects were presumed to use a 'conversion' method, thus making the negative sentences unusable for this purpose.

The first observation that one can make about these tables is that Negation Time

TABLE V. *Negation times for explicit full negation*

Source	Example of Negative Sentence Used	Negation Time	Falsification Time
Wason	Seven is *not* an even number.	550	260
Wason & Jones	Seven is *not* an even number.	440	420
Eifermann	Seven is *not* even (in Hebrew with *lo*).	736	67
	Seven is *not* even (in Hebrew with *eyno*).	600	232
Clark & Chase	Star is*n't* above plus.	685	187
	Star is*n't* above line.	709	155
	Star is*n't* above plus. (picture first)	556	148
	Star is*n't* above plus. (picture first)	660	145
Clark & Young	The star is*n't* present.	640	187
Just & Carpenter	The dots are*n't* red.	463	133
Wales & Grieve	Given 6 and 8, the next number is *not* 1.	455	140
	Median	600	155

TABLE VI. *Negation times for explicit quantifier negation*

Source	Example of Negative Sentence Used	Negation Time	Falsification Time
Just & Carpenter	*None* of the dots are red.	306	164
	There are *no* red dots.	76	218
	Hardly any of the dots are red.	385	167
	Scarcely any of the dots are red.	384	161
	Few of the dots are red.	210	263
Trabasso et al.	*KOV* green.	200	95
	Median	258	166

TABLE VII. *Negation times for implicit full negation*

Source	Example of Negative Sentence Used	Negation Time	Falsification Time
Clark & Young	The star is *absent*.	371	242
	The hole is *absent*.	185	291
Chase & Clark	*Absent*.	145	219
Clark & Offir	It is coming *from* town B.	184	155
	Mary has just come *out of* the kitchen.	201	150
	Median	185	219

TABLE VIII. *Negation times for implicit quantifier negation*

Source	Example of Negative Sentence Used	Negation Time	Falsification Time
Clark & Chase	Star is *below* plus.	93	187
	Star is *below* line.	135	155
	Star is *below* plus. (picture first)	117	148
	Star is *below* plus. (picture first)	84	145
Just & Carpenter	A *minority* of the dots are red.	241	96
	A *small* proportion of the dots are red.	214	240
	2 out of 16 of the dots are red.	72	31
Clark & Peterson	Star is *lower* than plus.	251	180
Clark	The pink one is *in back of* the blue one.	189	127
	Median	135	148

is positive regardless of the negative, although Negation Time varies from about a tenth of a second to almost three-quarters of a second. Falsification Time is also positive in all these studies. However, it does not vary nearly as much as Negation Time, but ranges between only about a thirtieth of a second to two-fifths of a second with the majority of the Falsification Times below a fifth of a second. Most important, there are no exceptions to the proposal that Negation Time and Falsification Time are truly positive increments.

The second observation is that Negation Times appear to vary systematically across types of negation, whereas Falsification Times do not. The median Negation Times order themselves from longest to shortest as follows: explicit full negation (600 msec), explicit quantifier negation (258 msec), implicit full negation (185 msec), and implicit quantifier negation (145 msec). That is, Negation Time decreases approximately from explicit to implicit negation, and from full to quantifier negation. In more detail, the explicit full negatives clearly have the longest Negation Times; its exemplars, which vary from 440 msec to 736 msec, do not overlap with those of any other category. Although the exemplars of the other three categories have considerable overlap with one another, there is at least a hint that the medians might be reflecting real differences among the latter three categories. In contrast, the median Falsification Times vary very little from category to category, hovering around 160 msec for most exemplars in the four tables.

This second observation, then, supports the scope of negation hypothesis, since Negation Times follow the scope of negation, whereas Falsification Times do not. Explicit negatives have greater scope of negation than implicit negatives, and full negatives have greater scope than quantifier negatives, and these differences are correlated with differences in Negation time. (It should be noted that the first two exemplars in Table VI are included there, not because they are truly explicit quantifier negatives, but because their scope is less than the sentence negatives in Table V and is approximately equal to the explicit quantifier negatives.) These data, then, constitute support, albeit less than overwhelming support, for the scope of negation hypothesis.

The second observation also supports the four Stage 3 comparison operations shown in Table II. If Negation Time can vary independently of Falsification Time, as these results show, then the mental operations that produce Negation Time must be separate from the mental operations that produce Falsification Time. Significantly, this is a property of the Stage 3 comparison operations of the 'true' model of negation. Operations 1 and 1a are quite separate from Operations 2 and 2a.

A third observation is that Negation Times and Falsification Times are relatively homogeneous within each table despite the wide variety of exemplars there. Take, for example, the explicit full negatives in Table V. The exemplars in this table include locatives (*Star isn't above plus*), attributives (*The dots aren't red*), and predicate nominatives (*Seven is not an even number*). The exemplars also include sentences in which only one word — other than the negative — is significant for the verification (*The dots aren't red*), two words (*Seven is not an even number*), or three words (*Given 6 and 8, the next number is not 1*). It appears that Negation Time is around 600 msec, and Falsification Time is around 155 msec, regardless of other incidental properties of the sentences: there does not seem to be any systematic variation in Negation Time and Falsification Time with, for example, number of significant words. If these observations are supported by future research, it constitutes evidence for the relative independence of Negation Time and Falsification Time from certain other attributes of sentences.

Summary data like these, of course, should be interpreted with a great deal of caution. First, the experimental methods varied considerably from study to study; in some cases, the experimental error was large, but in others it was small. Second, we have no idea how other differences in the negative exemplars — like the difference between *from* and *out of* — affect Negation Time and Falsification Time. Furthermore, we have only separated out the negative exemplars according to gross differences in scope of negation. Two exemplars within a single table might well differ in scope of negation in a subtler way, and by hypothesis, this should have an effect on Negation Time as well. Third, Negation Time can be significantly affected by the range of objects (e.g. pictures) that the sentences are verified against. Consider, for example, the three instances of *absent* listed in Table VII. The first sentence was verified against a picture of a plus ('true') or a star ('false'), the second, against a picture of an empty square ('true') or a circle within a square ('false'), and the third, against a picture of a disk absent ('true') or present ('false'). The three corresponding Negation Times, then, vary because of subtle interactions between the negative sentences themselves and the type of evidence they are compared against. Although I will discuss the reasons for the Negation Time differences in this particular example later, I am quite uncertain as to which experimental variations are important in the other exemplars and which are not. Fourth, Negation Times can be reduced with practice. Young and Chase (1971), and Singer, Chase, Young, and Clark (1971), who ran subjects for 10 to 15 days, found that although Negation Time began at 600 msec, it diminished to as little as 100 msec by the end of all that practice. Since the experiments listed in these four tables could also well differ in how practiced the subjects were (either on negatives in general or on the particular negatives of the experiment), some of the variation in these tables might be due to practice effects.

In summary, the support for the scope of negation hypothesis, though quite meager, is still suggestive. The most direct evidence is that Negation Time for *absent* is considerably less than for *not present* (Clark and Young 1971), and that the instruction 'Mark all the numbers except 2, 5, 8' is easier than the instruction 'Mark all the numbers but do not mark 2, 5, 8' (Jones 1968). Suggestive, but not conclusive, is the combined evidence from the existing studies on negation. They show that explicit full negation has longer Negation Time than explicit quantifier negation, implicit full negation, or implicit quantifier negation, and that the latter three categories might possibly be ordered in this way from longest to shortest Negation Time. In contrast, Falsification Times do not differ much from category to category. As yet, there seem to be no counter-examples to the hypothesis. Better confirmation of this hypothesis waits on studies, like that of Clark and Young, in which scope of negation can be varied without concomitant changes in verifying evidence, practice, and other confounding effects.

2.46   On the putative 'prohibitive connotation' of negatives

Other proposals have been made as to why one negative is more difficult than another. Eifermann (1961) and Wason and Jones (1963), for example, proposed that certain types of negatives differ in what they called a 'prohibitive connotation'. The first proposal of this sort appears to have been made by Eifermann. She claimed in her study that the Hebrew negative *lo* was more difficult than the Hebrew negative *eyno*. And since *lo* is used in all negative contexts, including the prohibitive one, whereas *eyno* is not, she suggested that the greater difficulty of *lo* over *eyno* might be related to *lo*'s prohibitive connotation which somehow makes it more difficult to process. Wason and Jones (1963), referring to Eifermann, then tentatively suggested that the difference between the two kinds of negatives in their study might also be attributed to 'an inhibition of response specifically associated with the prohibitive connotations of the word "not"'.

Unfortunately, a closer look at Eifermann's data reveals that Eifermann's conclusion of a difference between *lo* and *eyno* was quite unwarranted. In her study, one group of subjects received *lo* and the other *eyno*, in True Negative and False Negative sentences. But both groups received the identical True Affirmative and False Affirmative sentences. Eifermann's data show that, for some unknown reason, the group that received *lo* verified *both* Affirmative *and* Negative sentences an average of 325 msec slower than the group that received *eyno*. The important point here is that the former group was not only slower on the *lo* sentences, but also on the affirmative sentences that were identical for both groups. In spite of this fact, Eifermann concluded that *lo* was more difficult than *eyno*. The appropriate way to compare *lo* and *eyno* is to use Negation Time, as we have done in the above discussion. The Negation Time is 736 msec for *lo* and 600 msec for *eyno*, and from the statistics that Eifermann reports, the difference between the two is not statistically significant. What reinforces the conclusion that *lo* and *eyno* are not really different is that on another task in which subjects were required to construct true or false affirmative or negative sentences there were no differences between *lo* and *eyno*. One can only conclude that there is no empirical support in Eifermann's data for her proposal that 'prohibitive connotations' of certain types of negatives make them more difficult to process.

Given the present framework, one could also question Wason and Jones' conclusion that some sort of response inhibition could have served as an explanation in their study. Their study went as follows: They gave their subjects either explicitly negative sentences, like 7 *is not an even number,* or logically negative sentences, like 7 *med an even number.* The positive counterparts were 7 *is an even number* and 7 *dax an even number,* respectively. The subjects were to 'tick' true sentences and 'cross' false sentences, but for *med* and *dax,* the subjects had to figure out the correct system for themselves. Wason and Jones found that Negation Time for the explicitly negative sentences was greater than Negation Time for the logically defined negative sentences, which they took as evidence for the prohibitive connotations of explicit over logical negatives. But Wason and Jones also questioned their subjects and found that those subjects given the explicit sentence used either the 'true' or 'conversion' method of negation in verifying the sentence. In contrast, only a third of the subjects given the logical negative did so. Instead, most subjects in the latter condition rigged up some kind of decision procedure, e.g. 'if an even number and Dax, or an odd number and Med, then press "tick"; otherwise press "cross"'. This, of course, is quite a different verification procedure from either the 'true' or 'conversion' model of negation, nevertheless one that could be modeled by a process of mental operations. There is no reason to believe that the Negation Time should be slower or faster for the various logical methods. One can only conclude that, yes, there are several possible ways of verifying negative sentences, and the *med* and *dax* can lead subjects to use methods different from the 'true' or 'conversion' methods of negation. But none of these methods leads to the conclusion that the 'prohibitive connotations of the word "not"' are involved with explicit negatives.

The inevitable conclusion appears to be that there is no direct evidence at all for the hypothesis that the difficulties of some negatives are the result of a 'prohibitive connotation' of those negatives.

2.47 *On the 'contexts of plausible denial'*

In section 2.3, I argued that sentence negation as in *John isn't at home* is best thought of as consisting of a supposition — *John is at home* — plus a denial of that supposition. Furthermore, I pointed out that the supposition is normally something that is plausible to the speaker and listener; for example, *John isn't at home* would be said if it was expected, believed, or supposed in that context that John was at home. In other words, the supposition has to be plausible in context. By somewhat similar reasoning, Wason (1965) has argued in a very interesting study that negatives can normally be used to describe only the exceptional item in a set of otherwise homogeneous objects. From this standpoint, Wason proposed two hypotheses. The Exceptionality hypothesis can be illustrated as follows: In an athletic team of ten people, only one of which (player number ten) is a girl, it is appropriate to say *Player number ten isn't male,* but inappropriate to say *Player number one isn't female.* By this hypothesis, it is appropriate to select the exception for negative comment. The Ratio hypothesis, which is perceptibly different from the

Exceptionality hypothesis, goes as follows: For the same athletic team, it is appropriate to say *Exactly one player isn't male*, but inappropriate to say *Exactly nine players aren't female*. Although the present treatment of supposition and Wason's treatment of exceptions are similar in spirit, they differ at a crucial point. Where Wason would argue for both the Exceptionality and Ratio hypotheses, the suppositional treatment would predict that the Exceptionality hypothesis is valid, but the Ratio hypothesis is not.

Let us examine what the suppositional treatment would predict for the Exceptionality and Ratio hypotheses. First, consider the two sentences under the Exceptionality hypothesis, their semantic representations, and their paraphrases:

    25 a) Player number ten isn't male.
        b) (false (suppose (player number ten is male)))
        c) It is false to suppose that player number ten is male.
    26 a) Player number one isn't female.
        b) (false (suppose (player number one is female)))
        c) It is false to suppose that player number one is female.

Thus, underlying **25** is the supposition that the particular player being referred to is male, while underlying **26** is the supposition that the particular player being referred to is female. Since most of the players are male, the supposition of **25** is plausible a priori, but that of **26** is not. So by the suppositional analysis, **25** ought to be more in line with a priori expectations — i.e. congruent with expectations — than **26**, hence easier than **26**. Note that **26c** — *It is false to suppose that player number one is female* — evokes a sort of surprise reaction, 'But why do you think I would suppose that?'

In contrast, the two sentences under the Ratio hypothesis, their semantic representations, and their paraphrases are shown in **27** and **28**:

    27 a) Exactly one player isn't male.
        b) (false (suppose (exactly one player is male)))
        c) It is false to suppose that exactly one player is male.
    28 a) Exactly nine players aren't female.
        b) (false (suppose (exactly nine players are female)))
        c) It is false to suppose that exactly nine players are female.

Thus, underlying **27** is the supposition that exactly one player is male, and underlying **28** is the supposition that exactly nine players are female. But note that both of these suppositions are implausible in context. If most of the players are men, the supposition in **27** that exactly one player is male is contradictory to that expectation; *exactly one* has the effect of saying *no more or no less than one player is male,* which is not at all congruent with the a priori expectation. As Just and Carpenter pointed out, **27** is in a sense a double negative, with an explicit negative in *isn't* and an implicit negative in *exactly one* (like their *2 out of 16*). That is, **27** has the sense of the following analysis: *(false (suppose (players (false (players are many)) are male))),* paraphrased as *It is incorrect to suppose that there aren't many* *players who are male.* The supposition of **28** — that exactly nine players are female — is just as implausible in this context. Thus, the suppositional analysis would claim that the Ratio hypothesis is incorrect: both **27** and **28** should be difficult, since neither of their suppositions is plausible within the context of this particular athletic team.

In agreement with the present suppositional analysis, Wason's experimental results supported the Exceptionality hypothesis, but not the Ratio hypothesis. He found that sentences like **25** were relatively easier than ones like **26**, but that sentences like **27** and **28** were equally difficult. In his experiment, the subjects viewed and described a set of eight circles, seven of which were, say, blue and one of which was red; immediately afterwards, they attempted to complete an incomplete sentence ('Circle number 7 is not . . .') with the correct color as quickly as possible while they were timed. But I should add one note of caution about Wason's results. He had one group of subjects always complete the Exceptionality-type sentences, and another group always complete the Ratio-type sentences. Unfortunately, in the period just before they were to complete the sentences, the Exceptionality group tended to describe the set of circles with the exceptional item first ('Circle number 4 is blue and the rest are red'), whereas the Ratio group did just the opposite ('Seven circles are red and one is blue'). This gives us strong reason to suspect that identical pictures were encoded in two different ways by the two different groups. We know from previous experiments (cf. Clark and Chase 1972; Clark and Young, in preparation) that the form the coding of a picture takes in memory can have dramatic effects on the subsequent verification of that sentence. Although it is difficult to guess just how the encoding should have affected Wason's experiment, one should nevertheless be cautious in accepting his results as final.

Wason's results nonetheless appear to support the analysis of negative sentences into a supposition and a negation. To explain Wason's results simply by appealing to general properties of sets and their exceptions appears not to work. Instead, the correct and more general rule is: a negative sentence will be easy if the supposition of that negative is plausible in that context. The more general rule, unlike Wason's rules, allows us to bring together in one unified theory a number of results that would otherwise not be related to each other. As an alternative to Wason's correct, but fairly restricted Exceptionality hypothesis, the present suppositional treatment can be extended to other types of negatives, particularly implicit negatives like *except, excluded,* and *without,* which contain suppositions quite different from their explicit negative counterparts. The suppositional analysis, of course, would predict quite different results for the explicit negatives that Wason used and for the implicit negatives.

2.5 *Negation in Cognition*

As a final piece of evidence for the 'true' model of negation, I will now consider

several examples from perception that appear to require the present model of negation. Although perception has traditionally been kept quite distinct from psycholinguistics, it is obvious that there must be a representational system common to perception and language; otherwise, it would be impossible for people to talk about
pictures, to verify sentences against pictures, to imagine a scene as described by a
sentence, and so on. Indeed, as I argued in section 2.2, it is necessary to assume
that pictures are represented, at some level of processing, in semantic representations that are just like those of sentences. For example, a picture of an A above
a B is normally represented as (A above B), which is identical to the underlying
representation of the sentence A is above B.

The main point of perceptual representations is that they are normally positive
— that is, we code perceptual objects as positive entities. 'That is the Eiffel Tower',
we think, not 'That isn't Hoover Tower', or 'That isn't Coit Tower', or 'That isn't
my landlady'. The reason is clear. In most cases, there is only one possible identification of what a thing is, but many of what it is not. Yet there are instances
where it is important, and even necessary, to think of something in negative terms.
Significantly, the instances of negation in perception that I have found follow the
same logic as the linguistic examples of negation discussed above; that is, negation
in perception fits into the 'true' model of negation, and it can be analyzed in terms
of the supposition the perceiver has of the situation he is observing. I will first
examine evidence for the normality of positive coding, and then discuss a study
in which subjects found it necessary to use negative perceptual representations.

2.51 Positive perceptual coding

In the Clark and Chase study, to be discussed more fully in section 3, it was
found that a picture of an A above a B can be viewed in at least two different ways.
The subject can look at the top figure (A) in the picture, and if he does he will
encode the picture as (A above B). Or he can look at the bottom figure (B), and
in this case he will encode the picture as (B below A). When asked simply to view
the picture as a whole, the code will always be (A above B). In other words, an
A above a B is normally coded in a positive form — in terms of the implicitly
positive preposition above, although when the subject views the picture in a specific
way, he can code it in terms of the negative preposition below instead. Here is one
piece of evidence that pictures are encoded in positive representations, except under
unusual conditions.

A second finding of the same study is that subjects could not have been coding
the pictures as explicit negatives. A picture of an A above a B, for example, could
have been coded as (false (B below A)), which is a representation that is also true of
the picture. But the evidence showed that subjects did not use such negative codes.
Note that the use of this type of code would generally result in incorrect judgments
of truth value, for the above coding is consistent with sentences like A is beside B,
even though the picture is incorrectly described by such sentences. Negative repre-

sentations generally lose information that is contained in the normal positive code, unless that negative code specifies so much that it is unwieldy.

A third piece of evidence for the normality of positive codes is found in the *present-absent* study (Clark and Young, in preparation) reported above. There it was assumed that the pictures were encoded in a positive form; for example, a plus was assumed to be coded as (*plus is present*), not as (*false (star is present)*). The alternative assumption, that a picture is coded negatively, leads to incorrect predictions of the verification times in that study. So here are three simple examples of how pictures are normally encoded in their positive forms.

2.52 *Negative perceptual coding*

Although subjects normally use positive codes, it is easy to contrive cases in which they will be forced to use negative codes instead. Consider a picture of a square with or without a smaller circle inside it. The square with a circle is meant to represent the presence of a hole, while the square without a circle is meant to represent its absence. I have recently used these two pictures in a verification experiment in which subjects were given sentences like *The hole is absent* together with a picture of a square with or without a circle inside it and were asked to judge whether the sentence was true or false of the picture. In this experiment, the sentences describing the presence or absence of the hole were mixed in with sentences describing the presence or absence of a star or plus; the pictures for the latter were either a plus or a star.

The rationale of the study was that the pictorial presence of the circle would be represented as (*hole is present*), while the pictorial absence could only be represented in a negative way, as (*false (hole is present*)). Thus the *hole*-sentences will be verified against *either* a positive *or* a negative representation of a picture; in contrast, the *star*-sentences (or *plus*-sentences) will always be verified against positive representations. The representations for the sentences describing the hole and for the corresponding pictures are shown at the top of Table IX. They are to be compared with the representations for the sentences describing the star or plus at the bottom of the table. When the four-operation comparison process of Table II — the 'true' method of negation — is applied to these representations, the process still produces the correct truth value in each instance, but the latency components for the *hole*-sentences turn out to be different from those for the *star*-sentences. In particular, c never appears in the *hole*-sentences, and b and d are not correlated in the *hole*-sentences as they are in the *star*-sentences. In short, the 'true' model of negation predicts quite different patterns of latency for the two kinds of sentences.

These predictions are nicely confirmed by the results of the experiment. For the sentences describing the star and plus, the results were as usual: True Positives and False Negatives were faster, respectively, than False Positives and True Negatives. For the *hole*-sentences, however, True Positives and True Negatives were both faster than their false counterparts: in this case there was no interaction between

TABLE IX. *Hypothetical representation of sentences and pictures under two conditions*

Sentence Type	Sentence Code	Picture Code	Latency Components			
True Affirmative	(hole present)	(hole present)	t_0			
False Affirmative	(star present)	(false (hole present))	t_0		$+ d$	
True Negative	(false (hole present))	(false (hole present))	t_0	$+ b$		
False Negative	(false (hole present))	(hole present)	t_0	$+ b + d$		
True Affirmative	(star present)	(star present)	t_0			
False Affirmative	(star present)	(plus present)	$t_0 + c$			
True Negative	(false (star present))	(plus present)	$t_0 + c + b + d$			
False Negative	(false (star present))	(star present)	t_0	$+ b + d$		

true-false and positive-negative. This is just what the 'true' model would predict.

The experiment as I have just described it lacks an important control. *The hole is absent* was always confirmed by the physical or perceptual absence of a figure in the picture (viz. by the absence of the circle within the square), whereas *The star is absent* was always confirmed by the physical presence of a figure (the plus). One might argue that the difference in latency patterns between the *hole-* and *star-* sentences is attributable to the perceptual properties of the picture, not to the semantic representation of the picture itself, as I have been arguing. As a defense against this kind of counterargument, a second carefully counterbalanced condition was included in which *hole* was replaced by *lid*, so that *The lid is present* was true when the circle was *absent* from the square, and *The lid is absent* was true when the circle was *present*. In agreement with the semantic representations of the pictures, the *lid*-sentences had exactly the same pattern of verification latencies as the *hole*-sentences. The conclusion is that it is the semantic interpretation of the picture that is critical in this verification task, not simply the physical attributes of the picture.

In summary, the study with the *hole-* and *lid*-sentences constitutes one example of how a picture must be interpreted negatively and shows that when it is, the 'true' model of negation is still correct in predicting relative verification latencies. The negative interpretations in this study, furthermore, depended crucially on what the subject supposed the picture was representing. For example, the picture of a square with a circle inside it was interpreted as the presence of a hole when the subject supposed that the picture was meant to represent holes, but as the absence of a lid when he supposed that the picture was meant to represent lids. In short, our perceptual system makes use of negation too, and this negation is fundamentally of the same sort that is found in language: it consists of a proposition (e.g. *the hole is present*) embedded within another predicate (*it is false*) that denies the truth of the embedded proposition.

2.6 *Summary*

In this section, I have proposed a very general model for the comprehension of negatives. Basic to this model is the assumption that sentences like *Helen isn't at home* consist of two underlying propositions: the positive proposition *Helen is at home*, and the proposition *it is false*, into which the first proposition is embedded. In verification tasks, for example, it was proposed that *Helen isn't at home* is represented as (*false* (*Helen at home*)) at Stage 1, and its verifying evidence, say, that Helen is at school is represented at Stage 2 as (*Helen at school*). The Stage 3 comparison process of the model consists of a series of operations that compare the two representations. First, (*Helen at home*) is compared with (*Helen at school*), the two are found to mismatch, so a truth index is changed from *true* to *false*. Second, the embedding string (*false* ()) is compared with the lack of one ((), the two are found to mismatch, so the truth index is changed back from *false* to *true*. At Stage 4, a response is performed in agreement with the final value of the truth index *true*. This model was called the 'true' model of negation, and it was contrasted with several 'conversion' models in which negative sentences are 'converted' into positive ones before they are encoded at Stage 1. In a review of the psychological literature on comprehending negatives, it was then shown that the 'true' and 'conversion' models accounted for the main findings on comprehension time and comprehension errors in this literature.

Another important observation made about negatives in this section was that sentences like *Helen isn't present*, which contain explicit negatives, contain positive suppositions like *Helen is present* which are denied; in contrast, sentences like *Helen is absent*, which contain implicit negatives, contain negative suppositions like *Helen isn't present* which are affirmed. This suppositional analysis led to the expectation that explicit and implicit negatives would behave differently, and this expectation was verified in a number of studies on negation. This literature, in fact, suggested a hypothesis about scope of negation: the larger the scope of a negative within a sentence, the larger the Negation Time for that negative should be. A review of the negation literature was consistent with this hypothesis, although the evidence was not as complete as it should be. But the more general lesson was that it is imperative to take suppositions into account in constructing a model of negation, for suppositions were shown to be implicated in a number of studies on negation.

3. LOCATIVES

Another basic construction all languages have in one form or another is the locative, whose function is to describe the spatial positions of objects. In English, locatives normally consist of a nominal referring to the object whose position is being described plus a prepositional phrase, as in *The unicorn is in the garden*. The position of an object (the unicorn) is normally described only by specifying that position in relation to another position (that of the garden). This section, then, will be concerned mostly with the comprehension of sentences that contain prepositional phrases.

3.1 *Semantic Representations of Locatives*

The semantic representations of locatives must first take account of the linguistic asymmetries between A and B in sentences like (1) and (2):

(1) A is above B.
(2) B is below A.

Sentences (1) and (2) clearly refer to the same state of affairs, namely an A above a B, but even though they have the same denotation, they are not in fact synonymous. In (1), the position of A is being described with respect to the position of B, while in (2), the reverse is true. Why would one want to describe A with respect to B, say, instead of the reverse? One significant reason is that the speaker presumes that the listener already knows the position of B but not the position of A; therefore, the speaker will describe the position presumed to be unknown in relation to the one presumed to be known. Linguistically, this can be put another way: sentence (1) presupposes that the position of B is known. That this is true is demonstrated by the fact that *Where is A?* is answered acceptably by (1), but not (2), and *Where is B?* by (2), but not (1). The question *Where is A?* indicates that the position of A is unknown, and therefore, *B is below A* is unacceptable as an answer, since it presupposes that the position of A *is* known, thereby violating the implication of the question. Psychologically, the B of *A is above B* is a 'point of reference', and the sentence merely asserts that A has a certain relation to that point of reference.

Sentences (1) and (2) therefore cannot both be represented in the same form, say as *above (A, B)*. Rather, the proper representation must contain the information that one position is being described with respect to the other. A fairly complete notation might represent *A is above B* as ((position A) (above (suppose (known (position B))))), glossed as 'the position of A is above the supposed known position of B'. But this notation is too cumbersome to retain throughout this section, so I will use simply (*A above B*) as a shorthand for this more complete notation.

Even this representation is incomplete, however, for it does not fully indicate the relation between *above* and *below*. These two prepositions are not just two arbitrarily different prepositions in English but are converses: *A is above B* implies and is implied by *B is below A*. This fact might be represented for the present time by a featural notation, with *above* as [+Vertical [+Polar]], and *below* as [+Vertical [—Polar]]. The +Vertical feature represents all those verticality features that *above* and *below* have in common, and the ± Polar, a feature that specifies whether the point of reference is to be the lower or the higher of the two objects.

However, the analysis does not end here, since the features +Polar and —Polar have a far broader use than just the words *above* and *below*. Consider the four adjectives English uses exclusively for the description of verticality: *high, low, tall* and *short*. It is well known that *high* and *low*, and *tall* and *short*, are asymmetrical, with *high* and *tall* the unmarked or semantically positive members of the pair (Bierwisch 1967). An important property of these four words, however, is that they all refer to measurement from a reference point upward. *High* means 'of much height' or 'of much distance upward', whereas *low* means 'of little height' or 'of little distance upward'; although the point of reference for *height* is normally the ground, it is always below what is being measured. The analogous statements can be made for *tall* and *short*. Although English also contains the pair *deep-shallow*, which can be used for the description of measurement downward, as in *The ocean is deep*, *depth* is not exclusively a vertical measurement, as can be seen in *The cupboard is deep* and *Cushman went deep into the forest* (cf. Bierwisch 1967). More generally, *depth* means 'distance into an enclosed space from its surface' and is not related directly to verticality. In short, English presupposes that vertical measurement is made in an upward direction from a point of reference.

The property of upward measurement, of course, is a property of *A is above B*, but not of *B is below A*. This suggests that *A is above B* is the normal mode of description of two objects, and *B is below A* is the marked, or negative, case and is used only when there is some special reason to choose the upper object as the reference point. The notation that indicates that *above* contains +Polar and *below* — Polar represents this fact only if it is remembered that a plus is the unmarked, or positive, value on the polarity feature.

Psychologically, the unmarked or normal character of *above* vis-à-vis *below* leads to the following proposal. The representation for *above* is assumed to be set up in essentially one step, for the feature +Vertical always, redundantly, brings with it the feature +Polar. This redundancy rule would explain the normality of *above* over *below* and the fact that *high, low, tall* and *short* all presume measurement upward. On the other hand, the representation for *below* is assumed to be set up in two steps, first by setting up [+Vertical [+Polar]] and second by changing the sign assigned to Polar by the redundancy rule from + to —. A model such as this implies that *below* should take longer to represent initially than *above*, and evidence will be presented later that is consistent with this proposal.

3.11 *Properties of English prepositions*

A more serious representation problem arises when one tries to represent all of the English prepositions in a feature notation. At present, this is clearly impossible to do, and ultimately, it might well turn out to be the wrong approach. Nevertheless, it is instructive to consider certain generalizations that can be made about some English spatial terms, particularly since some of the generalizations are important for the psychological experiments that will be discussed. I will first outline a proposal that relates the spatial model underlying prepositions and adjectives in English to certain human perceptual processes. To describe and give evidence for this proposal in detail would go far beyond the scope of the present chapter, so a simple outline of the argument will have to suffice. I will then point out that certain other prepositions are found in positive-negative pairs.

3.111 *Quantifier negation.* English contains considerable evidence (cf. also Bierwisch 1967; Teller 1969) for the proposal that the semantic properties underlying English spatial terms are derived ultimately from the way we perceive the world around us. The main center of the perceptual world is the ego: positions are perceived in relation to the ego, as far or near, in front or in back, up or down, left or right, and so on. Normally, the positive visual field (the part that is normally visible) consists of the visible space that is in front of the ego and above the ground; the boundaries for this field are the ego for front-back and the ground for up-down, and the field is symmetrical about left-right. This suggests that perceptually the visual field consists of three fundamental coordinates — up-down, front-back, and left-right — and that upwardness from the ground is positive, forwardness from the ego is positive, and since left and right are approximately symmetrical, both directions are positive.

These perceptual facts have their semantic consequences. As pointed out above, verticality in English is normally expressed as measurement upward: *height* means 'distance upward from the ground'. This was also taken to mean that *above* describes the normal case and *below* the semantically marked case. These semantic facts, by hypothesis, are more or less direct consequences of our perceptual organization of the world, since upward is positive in the visible field. Distance in English is also normally expressed as measurement away from the ego. The sentence *How far is San Francisco?* in the unspecified case would be taken to mean 'How far is it to San Francisco *from here?*' The ego's being the reference point of the perceptual space makes this fact explicable too. There is also some indication in English that *in front of* is unmarked or positive with respect to *in back of* (in the same sense that *above* is unmarked with respect to *below*), since words like *backwards* and *behind* have negative connotations — e.g., *Little Eddie is backward* and *Mary is somewhat behind in her work* — whereas their opposites do not. This again is explicable from perception since forwardness, like upwardness, is positive in the perceptual field.

One can think of these properties in terms of negation. Objects in the positive 'perceptual field' are expressed in positive terms, whereas those in the negative field are expressed as implicit negatives of the positive term. In the terminology of section 2, *above-below, up-down, in front of-in back of, ahead-behind,* and so on are positive-negative pairs in which each of the negatives is an implicit quantifier negative. Thus the sentence *A is below B* is a 'weak' negative: it is not a denial, but rather an affirmation of the presence of a negative value on the *above-below* dimension.

In short, the hypothesis is that the semantic properties of the spatial words in English — e.g. *high, low, tall, short, deep, shallow, far, near, above, below, front, back, ahead,* and *behind* — are ultimately the result of how people perceive the space immediately around them. Although I have hinted only at the relation between positivity in the perceptual field and positive-negative distinctions in semantics, it can be shown that perception and semantics are very tightly interrelated in other ways too.

3.112 *Full negation.* As Gruber (1965) has pointed out, there are also three pairs of prepositions in English that contain implicit *full* negatives. Unlike *above-below, ahead-behind,* and *in front of-in back of,* which contain implicit quantifier negatives, *to-from, in-out,* and *on-off* contain full negatives. *John is out of the house,* for example, is referentially identical with *John isn't in the house,* showing that the relation between *in* and *out* is much like the relation between *present* and *absent,* as discussed in section 2. The positive and negative force of *in* and *out* can even be seen in such constructions as *Jane talked George into staying* and *Jane talked George out of staying.* The first sentence implies, positively, that George stayed, whereas the second implies, negatively, that George did not stay. *To* and *from* are the basic directional prepositions in English, and their positive and negative force can be seen in *John went to the house* and *John went from the house.* The first implies, positively, that John is at the house, while the second implies, negatively, that John is not now at the house. *On* and *off* are similar to *in* and *out.* These three pairs of prepositions, then, would be expected to behave very much like *present-absent,* since *absent* is an implicit full negative too, but somewhat differently from *above-below,* since *below* is an implicit quantifier negative.

3.12 *Time as a spatial metaphor*

In English, as in many other languages, time is normally expressed by locatives used metaphorically. It has often been noted, for example, that the spatial and temporal prepositions are almost completely co-extensive — e.g. *at home* and *at noon, in a house* and *in a moment, between now and then* and *between here and there, before me* and *before noon, behind the house* and *behind the appointed time,* and so on. The questions *When is the party?* and *Where is the party?* have much the same form and are answered in much the same way, e.g. *at noon* and *at home.* It can be shown that the temporal prepositions and their interlocking meanings are derivable from the spatial prepositions and their semantic field, so that what holds for spatial prepositions should also hold for temporal prepositions. The full explication of this proposal, however, cannot be accomplished in the short space of the present chapter, so this bare outline must suffice for now. The only reason for bringing up time as a spatial metaphor here is to account for *before* and *after* as temporal subordinating conjunctions and to predict how they should behave in question answering tasks.

The two constructions of interest are **29a** and **b**:

29 a) He sold his Cord before he bought a Citroën.

    b) He bought a Citroën after he sold his Cord.

As Kuroda (1968), McKay (1968) and E. Clark (1969) have argued convincingly, the conjunctions *before* and *after* in **29** are derived linguistically from prepositional phrases in the underlying structure. For example, **29a** and **29b** are derived from something like **30a** and **30b**, respectively:

30 a) He sold his Cord before the time at which he bought a Citroën.

    b) He bought a Citroën after the time at which he sold his Cord.

The sentences in **30** simply contain the prepositional phrases *before a time* and *after a time* with relative clauses attached to each time. Therefore, the subordinate conjunctions *before* and *after* reduce the prepositions and their subordinate clauses to ordinary relative clauses. Since the conjunctions *before* and *after*, then, are derived from temporal locatives, which in turn are 'derived' semantically from spatial locatives, it is quite appropriate to symbolize **29a** and **29b**, respectively, as the locatives in **31a** and **31b**:

31 a) $(S_1 \text{ before } S_2)$

    b) $(S_2 \text{ after } S_1)$

These representations are meant to be formally identical to the previous locative notations, with S_1 representing the first event in time and S_2 the second event.

The representations of **31** are better justified than they may first appear. First of all, if the sentences in **29** really are locatives as represented in **31**, then they should have the same asymmetries of presupposed known and unknown positions as true locatives. And this is so. Note that *He sold his Cord before he bought a Citroën* really asserts something like 'The time at which he sold his Cord was before the time at which he bought a Citroën', and presupposes both the sale of the Cord and the purchase of the Citroën. But more important, it presupposes that the listener knows when the purchase of the Citroën occurred. The time of the Citroën purchase is the point of reference for locating the time of the Cord's sale, so this is exactly analogous to 'space' locatives. Second, and closely related to the first point, the answer to *when* questions behave just like the answers to *where* questions. e.g. *When did John buy the Citroën?* is answered appropriately by *He did it after he sold his Cord*, or more simply by *After he sold his Cord* or *After the sale of the Cord* or *After four*; it would normally be inappropriate to answer *He sold his Cord before he did it*.

The temporal conjunctions *before* and *after* should therefore behave just like the locative prepositions *above* and *below*. The fact that temporal *before* and *after* are semantically derived from spatial *before* and *after*, analogous to *in front of* and *in back of*, respectively, suggests that *before* is implicitly positive, and *after* implicitly negative, and that *before* should therefore be encoded more quickly than *after*.

3.13 Summary

The semantic representation of a locative, then, is to be denoted simply as, e.g. (*A above B*). This notation, however, is shorthand for a number of facts that must also be represented in a more complete version of the notation. First, the position of B is presupposed to be known, and the position of A is being described with respect to B's position. Second, *above* and *below* are converses such that they differ only on the single feature ± Polar. Third, the representation for the positive word *above* is hypothesized to be formed in a single step, as opposed to that for the implicit quantifier negative *below*, which is formed in two. Fourth, prepositions like *from, off*, and *out* are implicit full negatives that should behave much like *absent*, another such negative. And fifth, temporal conjunctions like *before* and *after* are assumed to be semantically derived from their spatial counterparts and therefore predicted to behave like the latter — i.e. as locatives. I now turn to several studies of locative sentences in English in order to examine how the semantic representations for locatives just proposed fit into the theory of comprehension given in section 1. The tasks in these studies fall into three categories — sentence verification tasks, question-answering tasks, and instruction following tasks. I will discuss the three types of tasks in turn, showing how the theory applies equally to each of them.

3.2 Sentence Verification

3.21 Above and below

One of the most basic studies of locative sentences is the one previously discussed (Clark and Chase 1972) in which subjects were asked to verify sentences like *The star isn't below the plus* against a picture of, say, a star above a plus. That study demonstrated important facts about locatives: (1) the meaning of *above* is represented faster at Stage 1 than the meaning of *below*; (2) the verifying picture can be represented at Stage 2 in either of two ways; and (3) the picture is normally represented in terms of *above*, not *below*. These three facts are just what should be expected, given the linguistic features that were presumed to be part of the mental representations of locatives.

3.211 *Stage 1 coding.* In what is now a large number of experiments (Seymour 1969; Chase and Clark 1971, 1972; Clark and Chase 1972, 1974; Young and Chase 1971), sentences than contained *above* were always found to be verified about 80 to 100 msec faster than those that contained *below*. This difference appeared over all kinds of variations in experimental method, e.g. when the picture was looked at before the sentence, when the picture was looked at after the sentence, when the top or bottom of the picture had been partially obscured, when subjects were told to attend selectively either to the top or bottom of the picture, and so on. In Young and Chase (1971), subjects were required to change *isn't above* into *below* and *isn't below* into *above*. In accord with the other studies, whenever the *final* coding of the relation was in terms of *above*, that coding was verified more quickly than the other coding. This last result demonstrates that it is not the printed word *above* that is easier to perceive, etc., than the printed word *below*, but rather it is the coded meaning of *above* that is easier to form than the coded meaning of *below*; thus, neither reading time nor, say, greater familiarity with the printed word *above* can explain the *above-below* difference. In short, these results support the thesis that *below* takes longer to encode, to represent in semantic form at Stage 1, than *above*.

The only other pair of prepositions that has been studied is *in front of* and *in back of* (Clark, unpublished data). Significantly, sentences that contained *in front of* were verified about 190 msec faster than those that contained *in back of*, again confirming that the positive member of the pair is represented faster.

3.212 *Stage 2 coding.* A critical factor in the process of verifying sentences like *A isn't above B* against pictures is how one encodes the pictures. Consider an A above a B. Whenever people look at pictures like this, they find it difficult not to attend selectively to either the A or the B in the picture instead of to the picture as a whole, even when the picture is quite small. Whenever they attend to the A, it could be assumed that they are implicitly trying to encode the position of the A, not the B. In effect, they ask themselves, 'Where is the A?' the answer to which, of course, is *A is above B*, which describes the position of A with respect to some other known position in the vicinity of A. These considerations suggest the following thesis: people encode pictures in terms of the figure they have attended to.

What should their code be when they are not specifically instructed on how to attend to the picture? It was observed previously that in English the normal point of reference is at the bottom of the measured dimension (as in *tall, short, high, low*). This fact suggests that people normally consider the lower of two points as the point of reference and encode the upper point relative to this point. In other words, without any other constraints people should normally encode an A above a B as *A is above B*, or rather as the semantic representation underlying this sentence.

Indeed, the experiments of Clark and Chase (1972) demonstrate these two proposals about encoding pictures quite nicely. In one experiment, subjects were asked to look at the picture before they read the sentence under one of the three following instructions: (1) fixate the top figure in the picture; (2) fixate the bottom figure; (3) fixate the picture as a whole. Under instruction (1), the latencies of sentence verification were consistent with the picture coding (*A above B*), not (*B below A*), whereas under instruction (2), the latencies were consistent with the reverse. And finally, the pattern of latencies under instruction (3) was just like that under instruction (1), indicating that under normal attentional conditions, either subjects fixate the top and therefore code the picture as (*A above B*), or they simply look at the picture as a whole, taking the lower figure to be the point of reference. It was also shown that in instances in which subjects read the sentence before they looked at the picture, they invariably looked at the top of the picture whenever the sentence contained *above*, but at the bottom whenever it contained *below*. In doing this, the subjects were therefore coding the picture in such a way that the prepositions of the picture's code and the sentence's code were identical; this meant that they had less manipulation to do in the later comparison process in order to test whether the sentence and picture were in agreement or not.

Preliminary to another study (Clark and Chase 1974), subjects were simply asked to describe a picture of an asterisk either above or below a plus in their own words. Their descriptions were overwhelmingly couched in terms of *above*, or *over*, or the like. In the same experiment, subjects were also given pictures of an asterisk either above or below a three-quarter inch long line. In this case the asterisk above the line was described in terms of *above*, and the asterisk below the line, in terms of *below*. The line proved to be a salient point of reference, and, as such, it overrode the normal considerations of viewing the lower of the two figures as the point of reference. In spite of this asymmetry between lines and stars, however, it was found in the subsequent experiments that subjects still coded the pictures independently of these asymmetries when they read the sentence before they looked at the picture; when subjects looked at the picture first, in contrast, the asymmetries and their associated codings had the appropriate consequences on the verification process. This is accounted for by the fact that subjects attended to the picture in the sentence-first condition contingent *only* on the preposition of the sentence: look at the top if the preposition is *above*, but at the bottom if it is *below*, regardless of whether the asterisk is above or below the line. In the condition in which subjects viewed the picture first, many of them, when uninstructed about where to look, simply always coded the position of the asterisk with respect to the line.

3.213 *The Stage 3 comparison process.* We are now in a position to study the verification process of locatives in detail. The main principle that will emerge here again is the principle of congruence: the verification process attempts to manipulate the underlying representation of the sentence and that of the picture so that the two are exactly congruent.

Consider the sentence *A is below B*, which is to be verified against a picture of an A above a B. The following verification process has been confirmed by the results in Clark and Chase (1972) whenever the subject reads the sentence before he looks at the picture. At Stage 1, the subject codes the sentence as (*A below B*); at Stage 2, he looks over at the bottom of the picture, which he encodes as (*B below A*); at Stage 3, he merely checks to see if the subject nouns of the two sentences are identical, and since they are not in this instance, he changes the answer he presupposed to be *true* to *false*; and at Stage 4 he answers *false*. The manipulation he carries out at Stage 3 takes about 150 msec, making the non-negative false sentences 150 msec slower than true sentences.

Whenever the subject looks at the picture first, however, the process must necessarily be more complicated. First, he codes the picture as (*A above B*) and then he codes the sentence as (*A below B*). The stage 3 comparison process consists of two steps: first he checks the two subject nouns to see if they are identical; when they are not, he transforms the picture from (*A above B*) into (*B below A*); then he checks the two prepositions to see that they are identical; since in this instance they are not, he changes the answer he presupposed to be *true* to *false*. At Stage 4, he answers 'false'. What is important here is that whenever the picture is presented first, false sentences that contain *above* are processed with two time consuming operations, not just one: the subject noun-matching operation takes approximately 200 msec, and the second *true*-to-*false* translation operation takes 150 msec, as it did in the sentence-first condition. The significance of this process is perhaps not in the details of the comparison operations, but rather in the general principle that underlies these operations — the principle of congruence.

In summary, the studies on *above* and *below* confirm several a priori constraints on how locative sentences should be represented. The positive locatives *above* and *in front of* take less time to encode than their negative counterparts; pictures are normally encoded in terms of the positive preposition *above*; and the representations of sentences and pictures are compared under the constraints of the principle of congruence.

3.22 *To and from*

In a recent series of studies (Clark and Offir, in preparation), Carole Offir and I investigated the pairs *to-from* and *into-out of*, which contain the implicit full negative prepositions *from* and *out of*. In one experiment, subjects were required to verify sentences like *It is coming from Town B* against schematic pictures of a symbolic car (an arrow) pointing in the direction, e.g. to Town B and away from Town A. Among other results of this experiment, we found that sentences containing *to* were verified about 180 msec faster than those containing *from*. This is consistent with the hypothesis that *from* is the negative member of this pair of prepositions. In a second experiment, subjects were given problems like *John thought 'Mary has just come out of the house'; therefore, John could be in the house* ('false') and were required to say whether the conclusion was true or false of the premise. Again, sentences containing *into* were found to be verified about 200 msec faster than those containing *out of*. Furthermore, *out of* was found to behave according to the 'true' model of negation, since, in agreement with predictions from the 'true' model, an *out of* in the above premise followed by a *not in* in the conclusion was verified more quickly than *out of* followed by *in*. The second experiment, then, yields even more convincing support for the thesis that *out of* is comprehended as an implicit full negative, since the results here are similar to those for *present* and *absent* in section 2.

3.3 *Answering Questions*

The psychological literature has produced only two studies that I know of on answering questions raised about either explicitly or implicitly locative sentences, and they are by Huttenlocher (1968) and Smith and McMahon (1970). Both of these studies are important since they verify in quite some detail (1) the differences between implicitly positive and negative prepositions, (2) the role of the presupposed point of reference, and (3) the requirement for the principle of congruence. Before these studies are described further, it is necessary to determine exactly what is meant by congruence in a question-answering task concerning locatives.

3.31 *Congruence*

The two main questions that could be asked about the locative *John is ahead of Pete* are (1) *Where is John (or Pete)?* and (2) *Who is ahead (or behind)?* Let us represent *A is ahead of B* as in **32**:

    32 (A ahead of B)

and the questions *Where is A?* and *Who is ahead?*, respectively, as **33** and **34**:

    33 (A at X)
    34 (X ahead y)

That is, **33** and **34** are both simply locative sentences, but the location is being sought in **33** and an object (X) at some location is being sought in **34**. There is quite appropriate justification for these two representations. The question *Where is A?* is simply another form of the question *A is at what place?* (Katz and Postal 1964), which has, according to our notation convention, just the representation that is found in **33**. The question *Who is ahead?* is a complete locative, except that it lacks a prepositional object, represented here as y, simply because it is unknown to the questioner.

To see the effects of congruence, I must first outline the process of answering a simple question. In a task that will serve as an illustration, the subject is to read the sentence *A is ahead of B* and then answer the question *Where is A?* The subject would set up (*A ahead of B*) for the sentence, (*A at X*) for the question, and then try to match the two representations. In this case, the match is relatively easy, for the two representations are congruent except for the unknown but questioned location. The subject merely needs to replace *at X* in the second string by the *ahead of B* of the first, since all else is congruent, and the answer is therefore 'A is ahead of B' or more simply 'ahead of B'. What if the question had been *Where is B?*, that is *(B at X)?* Now the two representations — namely (*A ahead of B*) and (*B at X*) — are not congruent: the question asks about the position of B, but B is presupposed to be in a known position in the first sentence. To answer this question, the subject must first perhaps reformulate the sentence's representation, changing it from (*A ahead of B*) into (*B behind A*), then attempt to match it to the question's representation again. This time, of course, the (*B behind A*) and (*B at*

X) are congruent, except for the wanter answer; so *at X* is replaced by *behind A*, and the subject can answer 'B is behind A' or simply 'behind A'.

The answers to questions in English are typically elliptical, but only in such a way that the answer consists of the word or phrase that would properly replace the *who, where, why*, etc. of the question and make a full sentence. Thus, an answer to *Who left just now?* can be simply *George*, and this means *George left just now*; the answer to *Which table is Jane sitting at?* is *that one*, meaning *Jane is sitting at that table*; and so on. Note that for *Where is Jane?*, one must answer with a full prepositional phrase, like *at that table*, not just *that table*; the same can be said for questions containing *when*. The answers to *how* and *why* questions must be answered by phrases more complex than a single noun phrase also, e.g. *How did you do it?* *by jumping up and down*, and *Why did you go? because I felt like it*. The point is that because the answer to *where* questions must be a prepositional phrase (except for *here* and *there*), this indicates that the whole *at X*, a somewhat clumsy way of representing *where*, must be replaced by a prepositional phrase, like *ahead of B*, in the process of answering *Where is A?*

Now we must look at congruence in questions like *Who is ahead?* Consider the problem *A is ahead of B; therefore, who is ahead?* The sentence and question are represented respectively, as (*A ahead of B*) and (*X ahead of y*); the two strings are compared, found to be congruent except for replacing X by A, and y implicitly by B, and the answer is simply 'A'. If the question had been *who is behind?*, of course, the two representations would have been (*A ahead of B*) and (*X behind y*), which are not at all congruent. The sentence's representation would perhaps be reformulated as (*B behind A*), which could then be directly compared with the congruent (*X behind y*), and the answer *B* is directly forthcoming.

The principle of congruence, therefore, is capable of predicting which questions will be easy to answer and which will not. The four sentence-question sequences in **35** are congruent, in the sense in which I have used the term above:

> **35 a)** A is ahead of B. Where is A?
>
> **b)** B is behind A. Where is B?
>
> **c)** A is ahead of B. Who is ahead?
>
> **d)** B is behind A. Who is behind?

whereas those in **36** are not:

> **36 a)** A is ahead of B.   Where is B?
>
> **b)** B is behind A. Where is A?
>
> **c)** A is ahead of B. Who is behind?
>
> **d)** B is behind A. Who is ahead?

If it is assumed simply that each one of the extra mental operations required to make the sentences of **36** congruent with their questions takes time to carry out, then the sentence-question sequences of **35** should take less time to answer than those of **36**. This principle is confirmed in the following studies.

3.32 *Before and after*

Smith and McMahon (1970) have recently reported on an important series of experiments on the comprehension of sentences of the form *He danced before he sang, He sang after he danced, Before he sang, he danced,* and *After he danced he sang.* This series was apparently initiated in order to account for some previous work (Clark and Clark 1968) that revealed that subjects make certain systematic errors in recalling sentences of this form. In each of Smith and McMahon's experiments, subjects were required to read such a sentence and then answer either the question *What happened first?* or *What happened second?* The question was presented before the sentence in one experiment, directly after the sentence in another, and after a considerable delay in a third. In the latter two experiments, the subject was given the sentence, allowed to 'understand' it for as long as he needed, then required to press a button, at which time he was given the question or a delay followed by the question. This procedure enabled Smith and McMahon to measure sentence-encoding time separately from question-answering time. The pattern of latencies observed in these experiments was very complex indeed. One kind of sentence was consistently faster than another in one experiment, but consistently slower than the other in a second. Smith and McMahon rightly observed that these inconsistencies reflect the very flexible cognitive strategies subjects have for comprehending sentences; whereas one strategy is useful in one task, another is more useful in a second task. Smith and McMahon therefore proposed a model of comprehension expressed as a flow diagram with empty boxes that the subject could fill in with particular operations for particular tasks. Smith and McMahon did not explain what the possible strategies are or how the empty boxes are filled in for their particular experiments.

It appears, however, that by concentrating on the apparent inconsistencies in their results, Smith and McMahon overlooked several very important generalizations that could have been made. And these generalizations make good sense when the task is characterized as follows. The subject's first job in each task is to set up a semantic representation for the sentence and question at hand. To do this, he must note the particular surface structure of the sentence and use, probably, some heuristic devices in deciding what the representation should be. Just as Smith and McMahon observed, these heuristic devices can vary considerably from experiment to experiment. But what is probably constant from experiment to experiment is what the final semantic representation of the sentence and question should look like, and how long it takes to set up the representations for *before* and *after.* Specifically, *before*-sentences must still be represented as $(S_1 \text{ before } S_2)$, and *after*-sentences as $(S_2 \text{ after } S_1)$ no matter what the task; and the Stage 3 process of comparing, say, $(S_1 \text{ before } S_2)$, against the underlying representation of *What happened first?* should still follow the rules of congruence. Several of these generalizations will be examined.

First, Smith and McMahon consistently found that sentences containing *before* were answered more quickly than those containing *after*. In the experiments where they were able to separate the initial inspection time of the sentence from the time taken to read and answer the question, Smith and McMahon found that *before* took less time than *after* during the initial encoding stage, but approximately the same amount of time during the Stage 3 comparison process. That is, the *before-after* difference can be attributed specifically to the differences in their Stage 1 encoding time. This result, then, is exactly comparable to the conclusion reached in Clark and Chase (1972), in which it was found that *above* took less time than *below* to encode at Stage 1.

The *before-after* difference is further supported in Smith and McMahon's data when they also consistently found that *What happened first?* was answered in less time than *What happened second?* The representations for the two questions **37a** and **37b** can be represented approximately as in **38a** and **38b**, respectively:

37 a) What happened first?
   b) What happened second?
38 a) (X before (anything else happened))
   b) (X after (one thing happened))

That is, implicitly **37a** and **37b** contain *before* and *after*, or rather the semantic representations underlying *before* and *after*. Thus, if the semantic representation of *before* takes less time to set up than that of *after*, then **37a** should be answered more quickly overall than **37b**. This is exactly what Smith and McMahon found.

Second, the results of Smith and McMahon fully support the principle of congruence. Under the present scheme, *Before he sang, he danced* and *He sang before he danced* would both be represented as **39a**, and both *After he sang, he danced* and *He sang after he danced* would be represented as **39b**:

39 a) (S_1 before S_2)
   b) (S_2 after S_1)

in which S_1 is *he danced* and S_2 is *he sang*. The two questions *What happened first?* and *What happened second?* are represented as **38a** and **38b**, respectively. The sentence **39a** is congruent with the question **38a**, and **39b** with **38b**, while the other two pairings are incongruent. According to hypothesis, it should take less time to answer in the congruent cases than in the incongruent ones. This is equivalent to saying that it should be easier to answer with S_1 than with S_2 for the *before*-sentences, but the reverse for the *after*-sentences; that is, it should be easier in all sentences to answer with the event specified in the main, not the subordinate, clause of the sentence. This prediction is confirmed in all three of Smith and McMahon's experiments on *before* and *after*.

The remaining results in the Smith and McMahon data are not directly applicable to the underlying representations and their comparisons, but rather seem to relate to left-right heuristic strategies for 'scanning' and 'parsing' surface structure. And it was these remaining results that were inconsistent from experiment to experiment. For example, it was easier to comprehend sentences with the subordinate clause before the main clause in some instances, but harder in others; also it was easier to comprehend sentences with S_1 and S_2 mentioned in their true chronological order in some instances, but harder in others. Neither of these properties of sentences, however, is directly related to the final representations of the sentences and their comparisons, so these inconsistencies only serve to emphasize that the actual construction of semantic representations is quite separate from the comparison of two such representations at a later stage. In sum, Smith and McMahon's results appear to be quite compatible with the process of answering questions that has been outlined in this chapter.

3.33 Ahead and behind

In another series of experiments reported by Smith and McMahon, subjects were given sentences like *John is leading Bill* and *John is preceded by Bill* and were asked either *Who is ahead?* or *Who is behind?* The sentences were either active or passive and contained *lead, follow, trail,* or *precede* as the transitive verb. Although these experiments were even more consistent than the *before-after* experiments, Smith and McMahon still preferred the empty box model of comprehension. Here again it appears that stronger conclusions can be drawn once the task is viewed as a process consisting of separate encoding and comparison stages. Some justification is needed, however, for bringing up a study on transitive verbs in a section on locatives. The reason is that sentences like *John is leading Bill* contain implicit locatives. The questions *Who is ahead?* and *Who is behind?*, of course, are explicitly locative, indicating that what the subject must derive from his understanding of the sentences is their underlying locative information. The analysis I will propose for the locative nature of *lead, follow, precede,* and *trail,* however, should be considered only tentative until much more is known about the linguistic relations between words like *lead* and genuine locatives.

Conceptually, the sentence *John is leading Bill* seems to contain two parts: (1) the sense that John is directing Bill's movement or perhaps simply that John is doing something in relation to Bill; and (2) the sense of the sentence *John is ahead of Bill*. It does not matter here whether sense (2) is thought of as actually part of the sentence or as simply implied by the meaning of *lead*: the point is that sense (2) is necessary for answering the question *Who is ahead?* or *Who is behind?* For our purposes, then, *lead* and *precede* 'contain' the meaning of *come-ahead*, and *trail* and *follow*, the meaning of *come-behind*; Smith and McMahon implied as much, too, when they referred to the former two as 'come-first verbs' and the latter two as 'come-second verbs'. Thus *A leads* or *precedes B* contains **40**, and *B follows* or *trails A* contains **41**:

    40 (A comes ahead of B)
    41 (B comes behind A)

Furthermore, the sentence *A comes ahead of B* in turn contains (or implies) the sentence *A is ahead of B*, a simple locative; that is **40** implies **42**, and **41** implies **43**:

42 (A ahead of B)

43 (B behind A)

With the simple locatives of **42** and **43**, all the principles established previously for locatives should hold. The principle of congruence, for example, predicts that it will be easier to answer *Who is ahead?* for **42**, hence for sentences that contain *lead* or *precede*, whereas *Who is behind?* will be easier for **43**, hence for sentences that contain *trail* or *follow*.

Smith and McMahon's sentences also differed in voice, e.g. *John is leading Bill* vs. *Bill is led by John*. Although linguists differ somewhat in their derivation of passives, it is generally agreed that the same set of functional relations underlie both the active and passive. (Section 5, below, is devoted entirely to active-passive differences.) Thus, both of the above sentences have the same underlying propositional structure (*John leads Bill*), so both contain (*John comes ahead of Bill*) and both are subject to the same rules of congruence. But passive sentences give us a unique opportunity to compare surface and deep structure with respect to the notion of point of reference.

Consider the question *Who is ahead?* and the possible answers in **44**:

44 a) A precedes B.

   b) B follows A.

   c) B is preceded by A.

   d) A is followed by B.

As expected from the analysis of *precede* as *come-after* and *follows* as *come-before*, the question *Who is ahead?* is answered acceptably by **44a**, but not **44b**. But the passives in **44c** and **44d** pose special problems, for they are both relatively unacceptable as answers to *Who is ahead?* As we will see in section 5, **44c** might be paraphrased as 'As for the position of B, it is in a place relative to A'; that is, the passive makes the A the point of reference and this is in direct conflict with the point of reference in the underlying proposition (*A ahead B*). Thus, *Who is ahead?* and **44c** are congruent in their underlying propositions — (*X ahead y*) and (*A ahead B*), respectively — but not in their points of reference. A person trying to answer *Who is ahead?* from **44c** must therefore make adjustments for the incongruent points of reference and this should take time. It should be noted that **44c** with contrastive stress on B actually changes the point of reference from A to B and thereby makes **44c** quite acceptable as an answer to *Who is ahead?* **44d** poses an even more complex problem. Its natural point of reference, as a passive, is B and its underlying proposition is (*B behind A*). The person trying to answer *Who is ahead?* must first get at the underlying proposition (*B behind A*), but that should be difficult to do, since the point of reference of the passive (*B*) and of the underlying proposition (*A*) are incongruent. Next, the person must try to match (*B behind A*) to (*X ahead y*) and, just as in **44b**, this will require a transformation of some sort, perhaps changing (*B behind A*) to (*A ahead B*). To sum up, passives should be more difficult than actives, since to derive the underlying propositions a person must change the point of reference of the passive to match the point of reference of the underlying proposition. Second, **44b and 44d** should be more difficult, respectively, than **44a and 44c**, since the former require a transformation that changes their underlying propositions into something congruent with the underlying propositions of the question.

Smith and McMahon's pattern of latencies supports this analysis. The principle of congruence predicts that *Who is ahead?* should be answered quickly by the deep structure subjects (the logical agents) of *lead* and *precede*, and *Who is behind?*, by the deep structure subjects of *trail* and *follow*; the other four question-answer combinations should be slow. To put it another way, subjects should be able to answer more quickly with the deep structure subject than with the deep structure object for all four verbs. This is just what Smith and McMahon found. Furthermore, since passives have points of reference in conflict with the points of reference of their underlying propositions, they should be slower altogether than actives, and this is also confirmed in Smith and McMahon's data.

Ahead is positive with respect to *behind* in the same way that *above* is positive with respect to *below, before* to *after,* and *in front of* to *in back of.* It should be expected from the encoding hypothesis that *Who is ahead?* should be encoded more quickly overall than *Who is behind?,* and this too is consistent with Smith and McMahon's results.

If *lead* and *precede* are both *come-ahead* verbs and *trail* and *follow* both *come-behind* verbs, however, then the same principle would predict that *lead* and *precede* should be encoded faster than *trail* and *follow,* and this was not confirmed in Smith and McMahon's data. The failure to confirm would be serious only if *lead, precede, trail,* and *follow* could be completely characterized as *come-ahead* or *come-behind.* Obviously they cannot. As pointed out above, *lead,* for example, seems to imply a directive function of the leader in addition to its *come-ahead* meaning. *Trail,* unlike the other verbs, is derived from the noun *trail* and seems to emphasize 'being on the track of'. And *precedes* appears to mean simply 'be in front of'. It is unknown, of course, how the surplus meanings of *lead, precede, trial,* and *follow* affect their encoding times, so there is no reason to expect the first two to be necessarily faster than the second two. An additional problem is that Smith and McMahon used *precede* (like the other three verbs) in the present progressive tense: e.g. *John is preceding Bill.* For many people, *precede* is only a stative verb (cf. Lakoff 1966) and cannot be used in the progressive tense: *John precedes Bill* is fine, but **John is preceding Bill* is unacceptable. Of the four verbs Smith and McMahon used, *precede* was consistently the slowest, and it could well have been for this reason. The two words they used that seem most comparable are *lead* and *follow,* for *they* are converses in at least one of their senses. The two words in fact agree with the hypothesis: *lead* was found to be faster overall than *follow.* The encoding time of the verbs, then, could perhaps be construed as confirming the *ahead-behind* asymmetry, although the data are not without serious problems.

One of Huttenlocher's (1968) experiments on deductive reasoning further supports this analysis of the transitive verbs *leads* and *trails*. In this experiment, subjects were given problems like 'John is leading Paul; Paul is being trailed by Bill; therefore, who is first?' These problems contained all possible combinations of *is leading, is trailing, is led by*, and *is trailed by* and of the questions *Who is first?* and *Who is last?* Each problem was solved in two steps. The subjects were first read the first premise and were asked a question about it; then they were read the second premise and question and were timed from the end of the question to their answer. Unfortunately, since the latencies and errors of this experiment were reported only in a very abbreviated form, it is not possible to confirm all the comparisons derivable from the present theory.

Only four gross variations in the data are reported. In such problems, the first premise always delineates the ordering of, say, X and Y, as in *X is leading Y*. The second premise then must describe a third object, call it A, with respect to either X or Y, and this could be active or passive, and it could contain A as either the deep structure subject or object of the verb. The data are reported in terms of these latter four categories, collapsed across the questions *Who is first?* and *Who is last?* It should be noted that the second premise must always contain the middle term of the three term ordering – e.g. the term *John* in an ordering with *Bill* first, *John* second, and *Paul* third. Thus, for one of the two questions, the answer will be the A of the second premise, but for the other, the answer will be a term out of the first premise. If the answer is to be taken from the second premise at all, it will always be A, and not the other term. By exactly the same reasoning as in the Smith-McMahon experiments, the principle of congruence predicts that when the answer to a locative question — and *Who is first?* and *Who is last?* are locative questions — is the deep structure subject, that answer will be congruent to the question and will be easy to make; otherwise, the answer will be difficult. This is exactly the pattern of Huttenlocher's results. For second premises in the active voice, the premises with A as the subject had fewer errors — though no longer reaction times — than those with A as the object of the verb. For second premises in the passive voice, the same result held for both errors and latencies, with A easier as the deep structure subject — as the logical agent of the verb. Huttenlocher's results also verify the prediction that passive sentences will take longer to answer questions of than active sentences. Unfortunately, the difference between *Who is first?* and *Who is last?* was not reported. The present analysis would predict that *Who is first?*, because it would be represented approximately as (*X ahead of (everyone else)*), should be encoded more quickly than *Who is last?*, i.e. (*X behind (everyone else)*).

3.4 *Following Instructions*

3.41 *On top of and under*

Imagine a child sitting in front of a ladder-like structure that contains three compartments, one above the other, into which the child could place colored blocks. And imagine that there was a blue block in the middle compartment. The child is now handed a red block and is given instruction **45a** or instruction **45b**:

    45 a) Make it so that the red block is under the blue block.

       b) Make it so that the blue block is on top of the red block.

In either case, the child is supposed to put the red block into the empty compartment immediately below the blue block. The theoretically interesting question here is: Which instruction is easier to follow? Before looking at the results of this important study by Huttenlocher and Strauss (1968), we must examine how the present theory would answer this question, since this task clearly demands of the child that he comprehend a locative sentence in solving the problem.

This, and other instructional tasks of this kind, can be analyzed in two almost equivalent ways. The first way is to see what constraints are imposed on the task merely by the way the child presumably represents these two instructions. Ignoring the *Make it so that* for the moment — and Huttenlocher and Strauss show that one can — instructions **45a** and **45b** can be represented as **46a** and **46b**, respectively:

    46 a) (Red block under blue block)

       b) (Blue block on top of red block)

Instruction **46a**, like all locatives, presupposes that the position of the blue block is known, and it indicates the position of the red block with respect to the blue block; exactly the reverse is true in instruction **46b**. The task, however, is quite well defined, with the blue block already fixed, its position known, and the red block to be placed, its position unknown. Of the two instructions, only **46a** is congruent with the task so defined. To make instruction **46b** congruent with the task at hand, some manipulation must be performed. In short, **46a** should be easier when the fixed referent block is the point of reference — the object of the preposition — in the instruction.

The second way of viewing this task, and the one I will use from now on, is to imagine that the child is *implicitly* asking himself the question, 'Where does the red block go?' which itself reduces to 'Where should the red block be?' Because of its presuppositional constraints, this question is answered acceptably by **46a**, but not by **46b**. From **46a** and from the general process of answering questions outlined previously, the child can form directly, but still implicitly, 'The red block should be under the blue block' and hence 'The red block should go (or be placed) under the blue block'. From **46b**, the correct self-instruction can be formed only in a more indirect manner.

The first and second ways of viewing this task are almost equivalent, and they stem from the same presuppositional considerations. Both predict that **46a** will be easier than **46b**. The data of Huttenlocher and Strauss fully confirm these predictions. Instructions with the red block (more generally, the moveable block) as the subject of locatives were carried out more quickly and elicited fewer errors than the other possible instructions.

Unfortunately, Huttenlocher and Strauss' results are of very little help in determining exactly what subjects do on incongruent instructions like **46b**. The results of Bem (1970), however, are helpful. Bem found a group of four-year-old children who simply could not follow incongruent instructions like **46b** at all. These children carried out the incongruent instruction each time either inconsistently or consistently wrong. When the task is viewed as an implicit question-answering task — the second of the two suggestions above — then the children were initially unable to do anything but try to match the question *Where should the red block be?* and the instruction; they could not manipulate the situation further. So Bem tried to teach them how to solve the problem. Her procedure was to present another model ladder with the correct solution directly alongside the ladder the child was supposed to fix up; Bem would then read the instruction, remove the model ladder, and then urge the child to make his ladder look like the model as he remembered it. After this training, according to Bem, the child was able to conceptualize the problem by imagining what the solution was supposed to look like and by then placing the red block to fit this goal. In the end, all the children were able to respond correctly most of the time, although the incongruent problems always took longer.

From the present viewpoint, Bem's observations can be cast in a slightly different form. When the child is being shown what the final result should look like, he is probably restructuring how he should view the red and blue blocks: instead of thinking of the blue block as the fixed block, he can now think of the red block as fixed. He can then ask 'Where should the blue block be?' and although the child is physically moving the red block, he is thinking of where the blue block should be with respect to it. In support of this view, Bem found that when the child was asked immediately after placing the block what the instruction was, he replied most often with the instruction he was given, not with some transformation of that instruction. This view also coincides with an adult's intuitions when he carries out such a task. It appears, then, that Bem's results show that children do have to restructure incongruent problems; they do this not by transforming the instruction, but by changing the implicit point of reference in the final display.

The present model of comprehension would also predict that instructions containing *on top of*, a positive preposition, should be easier than those containing *under*, an implicit quantifier negative. Although Huttenlocher and Strauss' data were apparently not sensitive enough to detect this difference, Bem's results (personal communication) confirm this prediction.

The present view of the instruction task differs slightly from Huttenlocher and Strauss' explanation. In the account they preferred, the child is seen as treating the subject of a locative instruction as an 'actor'; and since the block the child has in his hands is also treated as an actor, the instruction is easier when the block in the hand is described as the subject of the locative. But this account gives no reason why the subject of a locative should be considered an 'actor'. It is not agentive, as the deep structure subject of a transitive verb is, and it clearly does not have to be animate. The attributes Huttenlocher and Strauss apparently want to ascribe to the subject of the locative are derivable only from the notions of (1) presupposed point of reference and (2) congruence. The latter two notions are clearly more general and more powerful than Huttenlocher's 'actor', for they enable us to view the difficulties of incongruent instructions as just a special case of the general theory of comprehending sentences, a theory that accounts for other facts about locatives, as well as facts about negatives, comparatives, transitive verbs, and other constructions.

3.42 *Push and pull*

In Huttenlocher, Eisenberg, and Strauss (1968), children were asked to follow instructions in a task identical in concept to the *on top of* and *under* study. The child might hold a red truck in his hand and have a blue truck in view in front of him. He would then be given one of four instructions:

47 a) Make it so that the red truck is pushing the blue truck.

    b) Make it so that the blue truck is pushing the red truck.

    c) Make it so that the blue truck is being pushed by the red truck.

    d) Make it so that the red truck is being pushed by the blue truck.

or the same four instructions with *push* replaced by *pull*.

Conceived of as a question-answering task, these *push-pull* problems fit quite nicely into the analysis previously given to the Smith-McMahon experiments on *lead, trail, precede,* and *follow*. The instructions of **47** — again excluding the *Make it so that* phrase — would therefore be approximately represented, respectively, by **48**:

48 a) (red truck cause (blue truck move)) & (red truck behind blue truck)

    b) (blue truck cause (red truck move)) & (blue truck behind red truck)

    c) (red truck cause (blue truck move)) & (red truck behind blue truck)

    d) (blue truck cause (red truck move)) & (blue truck behind red truck)

This notation, which views each instruction of **47** as the conjunction of a sentence with a motion verb and a locative, is only meant to be approximate, for *push* and *pull* have much more complex meanings than are represented here (see below). The main point is that a locative is at least implied by, if not directly contained in, such sentences, since *Where is A?* can be answered acceptably by *A is pushing B*, though not by *A is moving B*, which is not locative in such a specific sense. In any case, instructions **47a** and **47c** both presuppose that the position of the blue truck is known, and so are directly congruent with the question *Where should the red truck be?* The other two instructions presuppose the position of the red truck, hence they are incongruent with this implicit question. The prediction is, then, that **47a** and **47c**, in which the movable truck is the deep structure agent, should be easier than the remaining two. Further, the point of reference considerations that applied to *lead, trail, precede,* and *follow* apply here too, leading to the prediction that actives should be easier than passives. The results of Huttenlocher et al. and Bem (1970) together confirm both of these predictions.

Huttenlocher et al.'s data, however, appear to raise one problem for the presen¹ model. The claim has been made here that *push* implies the locative *behind* or *in back of*, and *pull, ahead of* or *in front of*. Under the assumption that *ahead of* is represented more quickly than *behind, pull* should be represented more quickly than *push*. But the results run exactly counter to this prediction. Other factors, however, seem to be at work here. The locatives *ahead* and *behind* underlying *pull* and *push* are really quite derivative, and seem to depend on our specific knowledge of trucks; people know empirically that one truck pushes another from behind. More generally, *push* means to 'move in a forward direction from the agent' (note the unacceptability of *John pushed it toward himself*), whereas *pull* means to 'move in a backward (vis-a-vis the agent) direction towards the agent' (note the unacceptability of *John pulled it away from himself*, at least without odd contrivances — I am indebted to Patricia Carpenter for these observations). *Push and pull*, therefore, contain the meanings *move forward* and *move backward*, respectively: the first contains a positive preposition (*before* or *in front of*) and the latter a negative. The assumption that positive locatives should be comprehended faster than negative ones, then, predicts that *push* should be faster than *pull*, in full agreement with Huttenlocher et al.'s data. Quite speculatively, then, it could be claimed that the most general meanings of *push* and *pull* do confirm the positive-negative differences in direction prepositions, in spite of the fact that the specific locatives derived from *push* and *pull* appear to indicate the opposite. Obviously much more linguistic and psychological work is needed either to confirm or to disconfirm this or any other explanation of the locative nature of *push* and *pull*.

3.5 *Conclusion*

In this section, it has been argued that locatives must be represented with at least two properties. Consider *Helen is in the garden*. First, the sentence must contain one object (*Helen*) — what the sentence is about — and its location (*in the garden*), which is normally expressed in English by a prepositional phrase. The prepositional phrase (*in the garden*) specifies a second object (*the garden*) as point of reference and a relation (*in*) that describes the position of the first object (*Helen*) with respect to the point of reference (*the garden*). Second, the mental representation of locatives must indicate that the position of the second object (*the garden*) is presupposed by the speaker to be known to the listener. That is, the garden is of little value in describing the location of Helen if the location of the garden is unknown.

With these two considerations in mind, the principle of congruence enables us to make several simple but powerful predictions about the comprehension of locatives. In verifying locative sentences, the point of reference in the sentence must be identical to the point of reference in the information being used to verify it; otherwise, the point of reference of the verifying information must be changed, thereby causing the incongruent case to take longer to verify. The same is true of answering questions. If the question presupposes the same point of reference as does the locative sentence being queried, then the answer is easily constructed; if not, one point of reference must be altered, and the answer takes more time to construct. Following instructions is just like answering questions. If the object that is to be placed in response to a locative instruction is not the point of reference of the instruction, then the placement is relatively easy; otherwise, the placement must be delayed while the perceived point of reference of the task is altered. In sum, congruence is required of points of reference in locatives in order to verify sentences, answer questions, and follow instructions; incongruence leads to a restructuring of the problem, a step that takes time and makes the incongruent instances more difficult.

Finally, it was proposed that prepositions expressing upwardness and forwardness are positive with respect to their implicitly negative antonyms; this proposal is based on the view that certain semantic features are ultimately derived from perception. As a consequence, the unmarked or positive prepositions should be encoded more quickly at Stage 1 than their marked or negative counterparts. This proposal was verified directly for *above* and *below, in front of* and *in back of, before* and *after, ahead of* and *behind, first* and *last,* and with considerable speculation, also for the pairs *lead* and *follow,* and *push* and *pull.* In addition, English has three pairs of prepositions — *to-from, in-out,* and *on-off* — that contain implicit full negatives, and here it was predicted that the negative prepositions should behave like other implicit full negatives. This was confirmed for the pairs *to* and *from,* and *into* and *out of.*

4. COMPARATIVES

English contains a number of constructions capable of making comparisons. The principal ones are the strict comparative (hereafter called simply the comparative), as in *John is taller than Pete,* and the equative as in *John is as tall as Pete.* Comparisons can also be made with prepositional locatives (e.g. *John is above Pete in intelligence, John is intelligent beside Pete, John has it over Pete in intelligence*), sentential complements (e.g. *John is too intelligent to go to college, John is intelligent enough to go to college, John is so intelligent that he finished college early*), and comparative verbs (e.g. *John exceeds Pete in intelligence, John's intelligence has increased, John is becoming intelligent, John is getting intelligent*). This list is certainly not exhaustive. In spite of the variety of English comparison constructions, psychologists have worked in detail with only the two principal constructions — the comparative and the equative. In this section, I will therefore consider only these two constructions and how they are comprehended. The treatment I will give will not necessarily apply to the other comparison constructions, since there are no a priori reasons to think that they are comprehended by exactly the same mental processes as the two principal constructions.

Psychologists have studied comparatives from three points of view. First, many have studied the more or less direct comprehension of the comparative, e.g. by asking subjects to verify or answer questions about a comparative sentence. As we will see, these studies are all fairly well accounted for in the present theory of comprehension with a few properties. Second, the comparative has been used to instruct subjects to do something, e.g. place an object with respect to another object. This type of task emphasizes a slightly different property of the comparative. And third, other psychologists have investigated the young child's understanding (and misunderstanding) of the comparative. The developmental studies, far from being separate from the studies on adults, actually help to confirm the model of comprehension proposed for adults. I will discuss each of these experimental areas in turn, attempting in each case to bring all the phenomena studied under one theoretical umbrella. Before discussing these three areas of comprehension studies, I will take up the representation problem, the question of how the comparative should be represented mentally.

4.1 The Representation Problem

The sentences *John is better than Pete* and *John is as good as Pete* have two very obvious properties. Both sentences contain two nouns referring to objects that are being compared, and the two objects in each case are being compared on a semantic scale represented by the adjective in the sentence. In line with the proposals made in Clark (1969a, b), I want to suggest that the comparative and equative sentences are best thought of as the comparison of two *sentences*, not just of two nouns, and that it is the two underlying sentences that make the comparisons either easy or difficult to understand.

4.11 Underlying sentences

Most linguistic analyses of the comparative demand that it be derived from two underlying sentences (Lees 1961; Smith 1961; Huddleston 1967; Doherty and Schwartz 1967). *John is better than Pete* is derived, ultimately, from something like that which underlies *John is so good* and *Pete is so good*, where *John is so good* means something like 'John is good to an unspecified degree'. That is, the comparative is derived from two sentences in which the adjectives have a 'degree marker' in front of them. The two underlying sentences are then conjoined by a series of transformations that insert *more than* (or *as-as*) giving, successively, *John is (more than Pete is good) good, John is more good than Pete is good, John is more good than Pete is, John is more good than Pete, John is better than Pete.* A similar derivation holds for *John is as good as Pete.* Note that whenever the adjectives of the two underlying sentences do not have the same sense, the second adjective cannot be deleted, as in *John is taller than Pete is wide*. And if the tense of the two underlying verbs differs, the second verb cannot be deleted either, as in *John is better than Pete used to be*. Ross (1969) has pointed out, furthermore, that the second sentence of the comparative may really be derived from a relative clause of some sort, as in *John is good to an extent to which Pete isn't*, in which the degree markers, symbolized here as *to an extent*, are shown explicitly. Although the details of the linguistic analysis still remain somewhat of a mystery, it is safe to say that the main outline of the analysis — that the comparative is derived from two sentences — is well-founded and this is really all that we will need here.

The two sentences that underlie the comparative can be thought of as presuppositions of the comparative. To say *John is better than Pete* is to presuppose that we can decide how good John is and how good Pete is, or that John is so good and Pete is so good, or that John and Pete are somewhere on the goodness scale. *John is better than Pete* can be paraphrased as *The goodness of John is more than the goodness of Pete*, or *How good John is is more than how good Pete is*. In these two paraphrases, the underlying pair of sentences is quite explicit: *John's goodness* is derived ultimately from the same structure which underlies *John is so good*, and *John is how good* (*how good John is*) is he nominal clause corresponding to *John is so good*. And like all presuppositions, those of *John is better than Pete* remain unchanged under sentence negation (Fillmore 1970): *John isn't better than Pete* still supposes that John and Pete are being compared on the goodness scale. This presuppositional evidence, then, confirms even further the more syntactically oriented evidence that *John is better than Pete* is derived from two primitive sentences something like *John is so good* and *Pete is so good*.

The only linguistic analysis I know of that does not derive all comparatives from two underlying sentences (Campbell and Wales 1969) is unsatisfactory, I think, on grounds related to this presuppositional evidence. Campbell and Wales argue that sentences like *John is better than Pete* should be derived from one underlying sentence, but sentences like *I like John better than Pete* from two. Their principal reason for wanting to derive the two differently is that 'in [a sentence like *The river is wider than the road*] two objects are being compared whereas in [a sentence like *The river is as deep as it is wide*] it is two properties, namely the depth and width of the river, which are being compared'. This assertion seems false on the face of it. The first sentence, *The river is wider than the road*, is just as much a comparison of two properties (namely, the width of the river and the width of the road) as the second one is. This information is explicit in the paraphrase *The river's width is more than the road's width* and is nicely captured in the two-sentence analysis. So one major reason for objecting to the one-sentence analysis is that its principal motivation is based on the very dubious premise that simple and more complex comparatives differ in what they compare. But there are still other reasons for objecting to the Campbell and Wales one-sentence analysis of comparatives. For example, according to Campbell and Wales, 'Putting it at its weakest, given two analyses of comparatives of roughly equal value from a purely linguistic point of view, we should like to see a willingness on the part of linguists to accept psychological considerations as being relevant here' (p. 219). As we shall see, the one-sentence analysis does not allow us to account for a large number of important psychological results that we will examine, whereas the two-sentence analysis does. So by Campbell and Wales' own criterion, we should reject their single-sentence analysis in favor of the more powerful and more general two-sentence analysis.

Now we come to the question of how we should represent the comparative and equative constructions. A fairly complete representation of *John is better than Pete* might be ((*extent* (*John is good*) (*false* (*extent* (*Pete is good*))))), which is to be paraphrased *John is good to an extent to which Pete is not*. For our purposes, however, it will be enough to represent **49a** simply as **49b**, and **50a** as **50b**:

49 a) John is better than Pete.
b) ((John is good +) (Pete is good))
50 a) John is as good as Pete.
b) ((John is good =) (Pete is good))

In these representations, the + is meant to indicate a degree or an extent greater on the *good* dimension, whereas the = is meant to indicate equal degree or extent. Sentence negation does odd things in this notation. The negative of **49a** is shown in **51a** whose representation is in **51b**; but since **51a** is equivalent in meaning to *Pete is as good as John*, the representation in **51b** is really equivalent to the representation in **51c**. The comparable relations hold for **52a, 52b,** and **52c**:

51 a) John isn't better than Pete.
b) (false ((John is good +) (Pete is good)))
c) ((John is good) (Pete is good =))
52 a) John isn't as good as Pete.
b) (false ((John is good =) (Pete is good)))
c) ((John is good) (Pete is good +))

The final sentence to be represented is *John is less good than Pete*, which is shown in **53a** with its representation in **53b**:

53 a) John is less good than Pete.
b) ((John is good—) (Pete is good))

The — marker denotes a negative rather than a positive degree.

4.12 *Underlying adjectives*

The full semantic content of *John is better than Pete* is not completely specified in the representation ((*John is good +*) (*Pete is good*)), for although this notation shows the synonymy between *John is better than Pete* and *Pete isn't as good as John*, it does not show the near-synonymy of *John is better than Pete* and *Pete is worse than John*. To be able to relate the latter two sentences, English speakers must know that the presuppositions of *John is better than Pete* — that John and Pete are being measured for relative goodness — can be translated into the presuppositions of *Pete is worse than John* — that they are being measured for relative badness. Although it is tempting at first to say that relative goodness and relative badness are the same thing, this conclusion can be shown to be incorrect. Our job for the moment is to specify how the goodness and badness scales are related and to write this into the mental representation of the comparative.

Evidence reviewed previously by Clark (1969a, 1970b) shows clearly that *good* and *bad* are asymmetrical. The asymmetry is that *good* has a neutral 'nominal' sense besides its more usual 'contrastive' sense, whereas *bad* has only the 'contrastive' sense. There are three main examples that illustrate the non-committal 'nominal' sense of *good*. First, note that the name of the *good-bad* scales is *goodness*, not *badness*. The term *goodness* normally spans the whole range of qualities from *good* to *bad*, while *badness* spans only the range from neutral to *bad*; *goodness*, however, can also be used in a second sense that spans the range only from the neutral point to the good end of the scale. Second, the question *How good was the dinner?* makes no presupposition as to the quality of the dinner: it could have been good or bad. But the question *How bad was the dinner?* clearly presupposes that the dinner was bad. The question *How good was the dinner?* with a stress on *how*, however, does make the presupposition that the dinner was good, and like the *how bad?* question, requests merely that the listener specify the extent of the quality questioned. So again, *good* can be used either neutrally or with a contrastive connotation. Third, although *good* and *bad* do not exhibit this quality, *long*, the neutralizeable member of the *long-short* pair, is also the member that is able to accept measure phrases. Thus, *two feet long* is acceptable, whereas *two feet short* is not. And *two feet long* does not imply that what is being measured is actually long; rather, it merely specifies that the dimension being measured is length, as opposed to depth or height or the like.

Putting this evidence together, we see that *good*, the positive term, is the only term able to serve as the name of the scale; hence, this sense of *good* — say, $good_1$ — might be called the 'nominal' sense of *good*. *Bad*, on the other hand, is capable only of specifying that something is below the norm on the goodness scale; it only can serve in a 'contrastive' sense. *Bad*'s positive counterpart is $good_2$, the 'contrastive' sense of *good*, as in *John is good*. The interrelations among $good_1$, $good_2$, and *bad* might be diagrammed like this:

$$\text{goodness}_1$$

$$\text{goodness}_2 \quad | \quad \text{badness}$$

$Goodness_1$ is superordinate to both $goodness_2$ and *badness*. Stated yet another way to say that something is $good_2$ or *bad* is to presuppose that it can be evaluated on the goodness$_1$ scale; similarly, to say that something is either *long*$_2$ or *short* is to presuppose that we can speak of its length. On the other hand, we can say that something has goodness$_1$ without ever committing ourselves to whether it is *good*$_2$ or *bad*. In short, *good*$_1$ should be thought of as the superordinate, or the semantically prior sense, of the two contrastive senses, *good*$_2$ and *bad*.

All this discussion is pertinent to the comparative, since it must be decided for the sentence *John is better than Pete* whether the *good* underlying that sentence is *good*$_1$ or *good*$_2$. In the evidence examined above, the only time *good* could take on the sense of *good*$_1$ was when *good* was modified by a degree marker, as in *How good was the dinner?* Other evidence seems to show that this is also true in general. But it was also noted that *John is better than Pete* is derived from the sentences that contain degree markers — as indicated by the *so* in *John is so good*. This means that *John is better than Pete* might be interpreted in two ways, one as *John is better*$_1$ *than Pete*, which presupposes only that John and Pete are being evaluated somewhere on the *good-bad* scale, and the other is *John is better*$_2$ *than Pete*, which presupposes that John and Pete are, in fact, on the *good* end as opposed to the *bad* end of the scale. On the other hand, *Pete is worse than John* must always presuppose that John and Pete are being evaluated for badness.

Now we return to the original problem: how can we translate from presuppositions about *goodness* to ones about *badness,* and vice versa? For us to be able to judge that *John is better than Pete* is synonymous with *Pete is worse than John*, we must know: (1) that *better* can be interpreted in the sense of *good*$_1$; (2) that *good*$_1$ is superordinate to or presupposed by *bad*; (3) therefore, *more good*$_1$ (*better*) is entailed by the expression *less bad*. It is clear that the relation between the two sentences is not a simple one, for in translating from one to the other, we are forced to choose *good*$_1$ before the translation can work.

The representation problem for *better* and *worse* can be solved, therefore, by specifying the relation between *good* and *bad* in the notation. *Good*$_1$ might be represented as [Evaluative [Polar]], *good*$_2$ as [Evaluative [+Polar]], and *bad* as [Evaluative [−Polar]]. This notation expresses the differences between the three senses quite accurately. *Good*$_1$ is simpler than *good*$_2$ or *bad*, since *good*$_1$ is not specified for polarity. Also, *good*$_2$ and *bad* presuppose *good*$_1$, since the former contain all the specifications of *good*$_1$ plus the additional specification of polarity on the *good-bad* scale. And furthermore, the translation rules for getting from *John is better than Pete* to *Pete is worse than John* can be written in terms of the simple addition or deletion of the sign in front of Polar. This notation and its consequences constitute what I will call the PRINCIPLE OF LEXICAL MARKING. Although this principle will be important in the following discussion, it will not be necessary to keep this cumbersome notation throughout. So it must be kept in mind that the *good* and *bad* underlying comparative sentences are not as entirely separate as the notation ((*John is good*+) (*Pete is good*)) might suggest; rather, they are identical except for the sign in front of the feature Polar.

4.13 *Model for the comprehension of comparatives*

A model for the comprehension of the comparative that has been proposed previously (Clark 1969a, b; 1970a) was designed to be general enough to account for a wide variety of comprehension phenomena. That model will be shown here to account for: (1) people's ability to answer questions like *Who is best?* asked of the comparative; (2) the relative difficulty of comparatives whose presuppositions are about *badness* (and other implicitly negative terms) as opposed to *goodness* (and other positive terms); (3) the difficulties people have in solving such three-term series problems as *If John isn't as bad as Pete, and Dick isn't as good as Pete, then who is best?*; (4) people's judgments of what is an appropriate paraphrase of a comparative; (5) the latencies people show in verifying true and false comparatives; (6) people's difficulties in following instructions, containing comparatives, on where to place things; and (7) the odd mistakes that children make in comprehending comparative sentences.

4.131 *Stage 1 representations.* The model simply asserts that the comparative in **54a** and the negative equative in **55a** are represented at Stage 1 as **54b** and **55b**, respectively:

54 a) John is better than Pete.
   b) ((John is good +) (Pete is good))
55 a) Pete isn't as good as John.
   b) ((Pete is good) (John is good +))

Also, the *less*-comparative **56a** is represented as in **56b**:

56 a) Pete is less good than John.
   b) ((Pete is good—) (John is good))

Another representation that will also be needed later is that for *Who is best?* Since this question is approximately equivalent to *Who is better than anyone else?*, it therefore has the same presuppositions as the latter paraphrase. For the present purposes, I will represent **57a** simply as **57b**:

57 a) Who is best?
   b) (X is good + +)

The two +s simply denote that the superlative degree of *goodness* is being specified.

Another problem of Stage 1 is how to construct representations for the underlying adjectives *good* and *bad*. The model presumes that *good* and *bad* are represented as *particular* feature complexes. The question is, should the two feature complexes be equally easy to form? Intuitively, the answer is no, for it seems that the unmarked or positive member of the pair (*good*) should be easier to represent at Stage 1 than the negative (*bad*). This would agree with the evidence presented in the previous sections on implicitly positive and negative lexical items: the positive prepositions, for example, were consistently found to be represented more quickly at Stage 1 than the implicitly negative ones. But if this is the case, how is this to be accounted for? In a previous paper (Clark 1969a), I proposed one model that predicts a difference in encoding time; in the present chapter, I would like to consider another possibility as well. I will call these two suggestions Proposal I and Proposal II, respectively.

Under Proposal I, comparatives with *good* are expected to be coded more quickly at Stage 1 than those with *bad* since *good* is normally neutralized in meaning in comparative constructions. The argument is as follows. By the principle of lexical marking, $good_1$ is represented in a simpler form in the feature complexes than $good_2$ or *bad*. The assumption is that since this is true, $good_1$ should take less time to represent than $good_2$ or *bad*. This hypothetical difference in representation time has two consequences. First, the *good* of comparative or equative constructions will normally be understood in the sense of $good_1$, since that is the simpler and first sense to be constructed. Second, and as a result of the first consequence, comparisons containing underlying *good* will be represented at Stage 1 more quickly than those containing *bad*, since the former will normally be understood as the simpler $good_1$ and the latter can only be understood as the more complex *bad*. In short, this predicts that comparatives with *good* (or any other implicitly positive adjective) will be encoded more quickly than those with *bad* (or any other implicitly negative adjective).

Under Proposal II, comparatives with *good* would be represented more quickly than those with *bad* because both $good_1$ and $good_2$ are represented more quickly than *bad*. The argument is similar to the one proposed to account for the difference between *above* and *below* in section 3. In this case, whenever the feature Evaluative is formed it could carry along no Polarity feature at all, and then it is interpreted simply as $good_1$, meaning 'extent of evaluation'. This, of course, should be the easiest to form. But, the feature Evaluative can also be formed carrying along with it the feature +Polar redundantly to form $good_2$, which is taken to mean 'extent of positive evaluation'. To form *bad*, therefore, it takes yet another step, and that is to change the feature +Polar to —Polar. The meaning of *bad* is thereby reached by forming the representation meaning 'extent of positive evaluation' and changing it to one meaning 'extent of negative evaluation'. Under this proposal, then, three levels of representation time are distinguished. First, $good_1$ should be the fastest, since it requires one less feature to be set up than either $good_2$ or *bad*. And second, $good_2$ should be faster to represent than *bad*, since the feature +Polar is set up redundantly with the feature Evaluative; and to form *bad*, the sign on that feature must be reversed in a further step.

As is clear, Proposal II actually contains Proposal I as one of its parts. Although the evidence needed to support either of these two proposals is very difficult to obtain, some results will be presented later that suggest that at least Proposal I is true. This evidence shows that an unmarked adjective that neutralizes is coded more quickly than an adjective that does not. But there also seems to be evidence that the positive adjective *large*, for example, is encoded more quickly than the implicit negative *small* even when the adjectives are not used in the comparative form and *large* cannot therefore be neutralized (Chase and Clark, unpublished data);

and there seems to be support for Proposal II in other unpublished data as well. The bulk of the evidence, however, is consistent with both proposals and cannot discriminate between them.

4.132 *Stage 3 comparisons.* In the present model of comprehension of comparatives, the Stage 3 comparison process is very similar to the corresponding processes for negatives and locatives. The main requirement again is that two underlying representations must be compared for congruence, and if they are not congruent, certain extra manipulation operations must be performed in an attempt to make them congruent. The main point concerning congruence that will interest us will be in the presuppositions of the comparative: if the comparative encoded at Stage 1 does not contain the same presuppositions as whatever is represented at Stage 2, then the Stage 3 comparison operations must make these two sets of presuppositions congruent before any other comparison operations can be performed.

Since specific applications of this model are easiest to describe in the context of particular tasks, I now turn to the experimental evidence on the comprehension of the comparative in four types of tasks: question-answering tasks, paraphrasing tasks, verification tasks, and instruction-following tasks. Evidence from all of these studies will be shown to support the main two proposals of this model of comprehension: the principle of congruence and the principle of lexical marking.

4.2 *Answering Questions*

4.21 *The two-term series problems*

One of the principal investigations of comparatives is found in a series of studies (Clark 1969a, b; 1970a) in which subjects were required to answer questions about comparative sentences. In the simplest of these experiments, the task is so easy that it seems trivial. Subjects were asked to answer questions of the following type: *If John isn't as bad as Dick, then who is best?* Here the *if*-clause (the 'proposition') asserts certain information, and the question immediately asks about that information. In these so-called two-term series problems the propositions contained *is better than, is worse than, isn't as good as,* or *isn't as bad as* as the relational term comparing two common names, and the question was either *Who is best?* or *Who is worst?* The subject was timed while he read and answered the question; his comprehension time was taken as the reading-plus-answering time minus the reading time alone.

This task can be viewed exactly as the other question-answering and verification tasks for the negatives and locatives have been viewed – as a four-stage process. Given *If John isn't as bad as Pete, then who is best?*, the process would go as follows. At Stage 1, the subject encodes the proposition as $((John \; is \; bad) \; (Pete \; is \; bad+))$. At Stage 2, he represents the question as $(X \; is \; good++)$; this notation specifies that the question presupposes the *goodness* scale, normally the *goodness*$_1$

scale, and that an X is wanted that fulfills the appropriate description. At Stage 3, he tries to match the question to the information in the proposition, and after a series of manipulations succeeds in replacing X with *John*. And at Stage 4, he utters 'John', the answer that has been produced by the Stage 3 manipulations. Clearly, it is again the Stage 3 comparison and manipulation operations that are of most interest in this process.

The main point about Stage 3 is that its operations obey the principle of congruence. Note that in comparing (X *is good*+ +) to ((*John is bad*) (*Pete is bad*+)), the first string is congruent with neither of the underlying sentences of the second string. The finding of congruent information, then, requires that the presuppositions of either the first or second string be changed. Let us assume that it is the question that is changed, from (X *is good*+ +) to (X *is bad*—), that is, from 'who is best' to 'who is least bad? Now there is congruence of the presuppositions of the proposition and question. By other minor manipulations, the question (X *is bad*—) can be made fully congruent to the subsentence (*John is bad*) of the proposition, thus making $X = John$, the correct answer. If instead the proposition is *John isn't as good as Pete*, and the question is *who is best?*, then the presuppositions of the proposition and question already match and there is no need for the first operation that reformulates the question in terms of the presupposition for badness. Therefore, Stage 3 requires one less operation — the question translation operation — when the presuppositions of the proposition and question are congruent than when they are not. As a result, the two-term series problems with presuppositional congruence should be answered more quickly than those without.

The results of the experiment of two-term series problems nicely confirm the predictions of this model. Table X lists the four types of propositions and opposite them the solution time, in seconds, for the two questions *who is best?* and *who is worst?* Proposition I was answered more quickly with the question *who is best?*

TABLE X. *Mean solution time for two-term series problems*

Form of proposition		Analysis	Form of question		
			Who is best?	Who is worst?	Mean
I	A is better than B	A is good B is good	.61	.68	.64
II	B is worse than A	A is bad B is bad	1.00	.62	.81
I'	A isn't as bad as B	A is bad B is bad	1.73	1.58	1.66
II'	B isn't as good as A	B is good A is good	1.17	1.47	1.32

and Proposition II, with the question *who is worst?* Similarly, Proposition I' was answered more quickly with the question *who is worst?*, and Proposition II', with the question *who is best?* In these four instances, the problem was solved faster when the proposition and question had the same presuppositions than when they did not. Furthermore, the surface properties of the problems could not, by themselves, allow us to make these predictions. For Propositions I and II, the answer was given more quickly when it was the subject of the sentence; in contrast, for Propositions I' and II', the answer was given more quickly when it was the predicate term. The main pattern of solution time, then, appears to be accounted for by the congruence or incongruence of presuppositions, as the model of comprehension predicts.

The comprehension model with its principle of lexical marking makes another prediction for the results in Table X — namely, that propositions with underlying *good* should be comprehended more quickly than those with underlying *bad*. This prediction is borne out with the comparative sentences, 1.10 secs to 1.50 secs, as well as with the negative equative sentences, 1.64 secs to 1.80 secs. Again other attributes of the sentences could not allow us to make this prediction. In the comparative propositions, the easier one, Proposition I, has the 'better' term as its subject, whereas in the negative equative propositions, the easier one is Proposition II', which has the 'worse' term as its subject. So again, solution time seems to be accounted for mainly by properties of the presuppositions.

4.22 *Deductive reasoning*

The second kind of question-answering task to be examined is one that would traditionally be included under the rubric of deductive reasoning, for it requires the subject to answer questions about the joint information from two premises. But it is really just a simple extension of the previous two-term series problem called the three-term series problem: e.g. *If John isn't as good as Pete, and Dick isn't as bad as Pete, then who is worst?* Although this task has been investigated by a series of psychologists (Burt 1919; Hunter 1957; Donaldson 1963; DeSoto, London and Handel 1965; Handel, DeSoto and London 1968; Huttenlocher 1968), the previous studies have made only minor reference to the linguistic processes underlying the solution of these problems. The model to be presented here, first proposed in Clark (1969a, b), makes the claim that the major difficulties in the three-term series problems are to be accounted for by the processes that deal with the comprehension and manipulation of the information in comparative sentences. That is, this task can be considered merely another example of how comparatives are comprehended, hence it should exhibit the same qualities found in the two-term series problems and common to other tasks involving the comprehension of comparatives. The difference between studies of three-term series problems and other comprehension studies is mainly one of complexity: there is a wide variety of three-term series problems that require detailed analysis before predictions can be made about their solution time. I will try merely to outline the argument, giving evidence from Clark (1969a, b) where appropriate. For a more detailed argument, the reader should consult Clark (1969a, b).

In Clark's (1969a) task, subjects were given 32 types of three-term series problems in the following form:

> If John isn't as good as Pete,
> And Dick isn't as bad as Pete,
> Then who is worst?
> Pete   John   Dick

The subject read the problem to himself and said the answer out loud as soon as he

TABLE XI. *Geometric mean solution times for three-term series problems*

Form of problem		Analysis	Form of question		
			Who is best?	Who is worst?	Mean
I	A is better than B, B is better than C.	A is good B is good C is good	5.20	5.80	5.49
II	C is worse than B, B is worse than A.	A is bad B is bad C is bad	6.10	5.74	5.91
III	A is better than B, C is worse than B.	A is good B is good, bad C is bad	5.09	5.58	5.33
IV	B is worse than A, B is better than C.	A is bad B is bad, good C is good	5.53	5.73	5.63
I'	A isn't as bad as B, B isn't as bad as C.	A is bad B is bad C is bad	6.96	6.25	6.59
II'	C isn't as good as B, B isn't as good as A.	A is good B is good C is good	5.84	6.61	6.22
III'	A isn't as bad as B, C isn't as good as B.	A is bad B is bad, good C is good	6.53	6.50	6.52
IV'	B isn't as good as A, B isn't as bad as C.	A is good B is good, bad C is bad	5.78	6.63	6.19

could while he was timed. Using the convention that the letters A, B, and C in each problem stand for the best, middle, and worst person, Table XI lists the eight basic combinations of propositions and their average solution times. Since the two propositions of each pair can occur in either order, and the question can be either *Who is best?* or *Who is worst?*, there are actually 32 possible three-term series problems — excluding, for now, those whose answers are indeterminate. The model proposed above makes several important predictions about the relative solution time of these 32 problems.

The first prediction to be made is based on the principle of congruence. This principle predicts that those problems for which the presuppositions of the question are the same as those of the proposition that contains the answer should be easy, and those problems for which this does not hold should be difficult. For Problems I, II, I', and II', then, this principle predicts that Problems I and II', which presuppose the *goodness* scale, should be easier with the question *Who is best?* than with *Who is worst?*, whereas Problems II and I', which presuppose the *badness* scale, should be easier with the question *Who is worst?* than with *Who is best?* As shown in Table XI, each of these individual predictions is confirmed, with an average solution time of 4.50 for the congruent problems and an average of 4.75 for the incongruent ones.

A second example of congruence is found in Problems III, IV, III', and IV'. First consider Problem III. The answer to the question *Who is best?* is A, which is found in a proposition that presupposes *goodness*; likewise the answer to *Who is worst?* is C, which is found in a proposition that presupposes *badness*. That is, the question and the proposition that contains the answer are congruent in Problem III. This is also true of Problem IV'. But for Problems IV and III', this is not the case. The answer, in both problems, for *Who is best?* is still A, but in these problems A is found in a proposition that presupposes *badness*; similarly, the answer to *Who is worst?* is C and is found in a proposition that presupposes *goodness*. Problems IV and III' therefore contain questions and corresponding propositions that are incongruent in their presuppositions. Solving Problems IV and III', then, requires an extra step for translating the presupposition of the question into one that is congruent with a proposition, and so Problems IV and III' should be solved more slowly, respectively, than Problems III and IV'. The solution times in Table XI confirm this prediction.

Finally, the solution times in Table XI confirm the prediction made by the principle of lexical marking that comparatives that presuppose *goodness* should be solved faster than those that presuppose *badness*. Since Problems III, IV, III', and IV' contain both a *good-* and a *bad-*proposition, they are irrelevant to this prediction. But Problem I presupposes *goodness* and Problem II *badness* although they are otherwise identical, so this hypothesis would predict Problem I to be solved faster than Problem II. And this is confirmed. .For the same reasons Problem II' should be solved more quickly than Problem I', and that prediction is also confirmed. The model of comprehension of the comparative, therefore, is fully consistent with the results from this set of three-term series problems.

In a slightly different experiment (Clark 1969b), the same three-term series problems were solved by another group of subjects who were given 10 seconds to solve each problem. For this task the difficulty of each problem was measured by the number of subjects who made an error on that problem by the end of the 10 second period. As one might expect, the results in this second task only confirmed what was found in the first: those problems that were solved faster in the first task were solved correctly more often in the second task. Thus, this second experiment fully confirms all the predictions made for the first. But this second experiment is of additional interest because subjects solved 32 *indeterminate* problems in addition to the 32 determinate problems shown in Table XI. One such indeterminate problem is *If John is better than Pete, and Dick is better than Pete, then who is best?* In this example, both John and Dick are better than Pete, and there is no way of determining who is best. The correct answer to this problem is 'can't tell', which was an alternative the subjects were allowed to give. The interest in these problems is not so much in their difficulty as in the mistakes the subjects made on them, for the model that we have been discussing makes quite specific predictions about what those errors should be.

TABLE XII. *Two types of indeterminate problems and their percentage errors*

Problem		Analysis	Principal Errors
	If G is better than J	G is good	G: 26%
VII	And J is worse than H	H is bad	H: 6%
	Then who is best?	J is good, bad	J: 2%
	If G isn't as bad as J	G is bad	G: 12%
VII'	And J isn't as good as H	H is good	H: 30%
	Then who is best?	J is good, bad	J: 2%

The errors are best illustrated in the indeterminate problems containing one proposition that presupposes *goodness* and one that presupposes *badness*. Two such problems, labeled VII and VII', are shown in Table XII. To see what errors subjects should make on these two problems, consider the underlying presuppositions of their premises; these presuppositions are shown in the second column of Table XII. In VII, we find *G is good, H is bad*, and *J is both good and bad*. In VII', however, which is simply VII with *is better than* replaced by *isn't as bad as*, and *is worse than* replaced by *isn't as good as*, we find that the case is reversed; now *G is bad, H is good*, and *J is both good and bad*. When the subject is asked to search through the Stage 1 representations of the premises to find an answer for *Who is best?* (i.e. (X is good$++$)), he will naturally search for an answer in a premise with a presupposition that is congruent with the question (i.e. a premise with presuppositions containing *good*). In VII, this strategy should lead the subject to find G, since *G is good* is congruent with $(X \text{ is good} + +)$, whereas *H is bad* is not. In XII', the strategy would lead the subject to answer H, since *H is good* is the congruent string while *G is bad* is not. The correct answer to both problems, of course, is 'can't tell'. Significantly, this strategy predicts the errors the subjects made quite accurately. As shown in Table XII, on VII subjects chose the incorrect but congruent answer G 26% of the time, but chose the other two incorrect and incongruent answers H and J a total of only 8% of the time. In VII', on the other hand, subjects gave the incorrect but congruent answer H 30% of the time, but the incorrect and incongruent answers G and J a total of only 14% of the time. Thus, the strategy of searching through the Stage 1 semantic representations for congruent representations strongly predicts the specific errors subjects made in those two problems. The other problems with the same properties as VII and VII' confirmed the predictions in precisely the same way (cf. Clark 1969b: 211).

In the experiments on deductive reasoning discussed so far, the principle of lexical marking — that positive adjectives should be comprehended faster than negative ones — has had only one piece of confirming evidence, namely, that comparatives with *good* were comprehended faster than ones with *bad*. But in sifting through the past literature on the three-term series problem, I have turned up many other examples of positive-negative pairs of comparative adjectives and their relative difficulty of comprehension. In particular, the data of Burt (1919), Hunter (1957), DeSoto et al. (1965), Flores d'Arcais (1966), Handel et al. (1968), Huttenlocher (1968) and Clark (1969a) show that the positive adjectives *better, faster, warmer, higher, deeper, more, farther, taller, happier*, and *older* are comprehended more easily, respectively, than their negative counterparts *worse, cooler, lower, shallower, less, nearer, shorter, sadder*, and *younger*. I have not found a single exception to this generalization in the psychological literature or in my own unpublished studies with various adjectives.

Jones (1970), moreover, has made some specific tests of Proposal I of the principle of lexical marking. As she pointed out, *heavy* and *light* are semantically unmarked and marked, respectively, whereas *dark* and *light* are not asymmetrical in this respect; note that neither *darkness* nor *lightness* is really the proper scale name for the *light-dark* dimension, particularly when applied to hair color, and neither *dark* nor *light* neutralizes in *How dark?* type questions. Similarly, *thick* and *thin* are semantically unmarked and marked, respectively, whereas *fat* and *thin* are not. If Proposal I is correct, therefore, *heavier* should be easier than *lighter*, and *thicker* should be easier than *thinner*, whereas there should be little or no difference between *darker* and *lighter*, and between *fatter* and *thinner*. These predictions were confirmed by subjects who solved three-term series problems as they were timed. So with the evidence from the previous literature and from Jones, there is very strong support for the principle of lexical marking.

4.23 *Psychophysical judgments*

Remotely related as they might seem, several studies on the psychophysical judgments of the relative brightness of lights lend even more support to the present model of the comparative. In the principal experiment, Audley and Wallis (1964) simultaneously presented two very bright lights, with one slightly brighter than the other, or two very dim lights, again with one slightly brighter than the other, and asked subjects to judge either which was brighter or which was dimmer. The subjects were timed from the presentation of the left and right light patches to the press of the corresponding left or right button. Audley and Wallis found that subjects could judge which was brighter faster for the very bright patches than for the very dim ones, but which was dimmer faster for the very dim patches than for the very bright ones.

With only one added assumption, this result fits quite nicely into the present conception of the comparative. The assumption is that the pair of bright patches are encoded as something like ((*left is bright*+) (*right is bright*)) — thereby encoding the comparative brightness of the left and right patches — and that the very dim patches are encoded as ((*left is dim*+) (*right is dim*)). The questions *Which is brighter?* and *Which is dimmer?*, of course, are encoded, respectively, as something like (*X is bright*+) and (*X is dim*+). The *brighter*-question, then, is congruent in its presuppositions with the encoding of the pair of bright patches, and the *dimmer*-question, with the dim patches, so the principle of congruence applies and predicts the differences that Audley and Wallis found. It should be noted that Wallis and Audley (1964) carried out almost the same experiment for high and low tones with the same results, and Shipley, Norris, and Roberts (1946) found similar results for comparative judgments of good and bad esthetic objects. Further manipulations of the stimuli also produced data consonant with the principle of congruence.

4.3 *Paraphrasing*

The second kind of study included in the broad category of comprehending comparatives is illustrated by Flores d'Arcais's (1966) important study on paraphrases of comparative sentences. Flores d'Arcais, too, noted that the interpretation of comparative sentences was influenced by their presuppositions — although he did not use the term presupposition. He noted, for example, that *Lambs are less ferocious than lions* seems to make assumptions about the underlying dimension that were different from those in *Lambs are more gentle than lions* but almost the same as those in *Lambs aren't as ferocious as lions*. In this paraphrase experiment, then, he asked subjects which of several sentences was the best paraphrase of sentences like *Lambs are less ferocious than lions*. His results may be simply stated in terms of the present model of the comparative. A paraphrase was judged more acceptable when it contained the same presuppositions as the target sentence. *Lambs are less ferocious than lions*, for example, since it is represented mentally as ((*lambs are ferocious* —) (*lions are ferocious*)), was judged more similar to *Lambs aren't as ferocious as lions*, ((*lambs are ferocious*) (*lions are ferocious+*)), than to *Lambs are more gentle than lions*, ((*lambs are gentle+*) (*lions are gentle*)). Flores d'Arcais's results re-affirm the conclusion that subjects derive and use an abstract representation of the comparative sentence that is something like ((*lions are ferocious+*) (*lambs are ferocious*)).

4.4 Sentence Verification

The comparative has been used in only one study of sentence verification that I know of, and that is one by Flores d'Arcais (1966). He was interested in studying the comparative adjectives *more* and *less*, since it appeared to him that *less* was psychologically more complex than *more*. Flores d'Arcais's task was an elegantly simple one. He gave his subjects sentences like *A lion is less ferocious than a sheep* and asked them to indicate whether the sentences were true or false as fast as they could by pressing one of two buttons. Flores d'Arcais timed his subjects from the presentation of the sentence to the response. Table XIII lists the four types of sentences Flores d'Arcais used, an example of each type of sentence, and the verification time for each type.

TABLE XIII. *Geometric mean verification times for comparative sentences* (from Flores d'Arcais 1966)

Type of Sentence	Example of Sentence	Verification Times
True More	A lion is more ferocious than a sheep.	2.68 sec
False More	A lion is more peaceful than a sheep.	2.90
True Less	A lion is less peaceful than a sheep.	3.53
False Less	A lion is less ferocious than a sheep.	3.75

In suggesting one explanation for these results, Flores d'Arcais hypothesized 'that the subject has to formulate the *right* assertion before reaching the decision. For example, when given the statement "A lion is more peaceful than a sheep", the subject would have to "formulate" one of the two following statements: "A lion is more ferocious than a sheep"; or "A sheep is more peaceful than a lion", that is, a true statement, and *match* it with the one given, to reach the conclusion that the statement is false' (p. 12). This suggestion is quite consistent with the present theory of comprehension, although it is instructive to spell out this model in more detail.

In the present theory, the sentence *A lion is more peaceful than a sheep* would be represented at Stage 1 as in **58**:

58   ((lion is peaceful +) (sheep is peaceful))

The critical question, however, is how one's knowledge about lions and sheep are represented at Stage 2. One possibility is that the subject accepts the presuppositions given in the sentence and attempts to express his knowledge in accord with those presuppositions, as in **59**:

59   ((lion is peaceful —) (sheep is peaceful))

At Stage 3, these two representations would be compared, and since they are congruent in their underlying presuppositions, this is easily done by simply comparing the + and the — (or the equivalent). A mismatch is found, the subject changes a presupposed truth index from *true* to *false* (just as with negatives — cf. section 2), and the outcome, *false* thereby serves as a basis for a push of the 'false' button. Under this model, false sentences should take longer than true ones, no matter whether the sentence contains *more* or *less*. Flores d'Arcais's data are consistent with this, showing that false sentences take 220 msec longer than true ones for both *more* and *less* sentences. Furthermore, since *more* is positive and *less* implicitly negative, *more* should take less time to code at Stage 1 than *less*, thus making the *more* sentences take less time overall than *less* sentences. Flores d'Arcais's data are consistent with this prediction too, showing a 850 msec difference between *more* and *less*. Unfortunately, this 850 msec seems considerably longer than 200 to 300 msec Negation Time shown for the other implicit negatives in section 2, and this suggests that there might be something additional that differentiates the *more* and *less* statements. What this might be remains to be seen.

Flores d'Arcais's data, however, allow us to reject certain other models as to how this comparison process might proceed. The most interesting of the alternative but incorrect models is one in which the subject sets up his Stage 2 representation INDEPENDENTLY of his Stage 1 representation. Consider the case in which the subject has set up representation **58** at Stage 1, and at Stage 2, he sets up representation **60**, which is true statement about the relative ferocity of lions and sheep:

60   ((lion is ferocious +) (sheep is ferocious))

In this case, the underlying presuppositions of **60** and **58** are incongruent, so the subject would have to carry out some manipulation to make them congruent; after that manipulation, he would find a mismatch of the + and — in the resulting pair of strings and would change his presupposed truth value *true* to *false*, as usual. If carried through in detail, however, this analysis predicts that the difference between True Less and False Less verification times should be smaller or even the reverse of the difference between True More and False More verification times. The data in Table XIII are not at all consistent with this model. It should be noted that the model just presented is similar to considering the True More, False More, True Less, and False Less sentences to be equivalent to *A lion is ferocious, A lion is peaceful, A lion isn't peaceful,* and *A lion isn't ferocious,* respectively, that is, as equivalent to True Positive, False Positive, True Negative, and False Negative sentences. The 'true' model of negation, it will be recalled, predicts that True Negatives should be slower than False Negatives, and this is inconsistent with the alternative interpretation just given of Flores d'Arcais's data.

This second incorrect model demonstrates very nicely how important the underlying presuppositions of the comparative are. In this model, it is assumed that the subject at Stage 2 set up representation **60**, which is a true description of the relative ferocity of lions and sheep. But how did the subject know to represent their relative ferocity rather than their relative laziness, their relative size, their relative speed, or the like? To have done this the subject must already have taken into account the presuppositions of peacefulness in the original sentence (in this case **58**); he would have had to have known that presuppositions about ferocity can be translated into presuppositions about peacefulness, whereas presuppositions about laziness, size, speed, and the like cannot. In other words, it is simply not possible for a subject to set up a Stage 2 representation independently of the presuppositions of the Stage 1 representation and guarantee the possibility of deriving an answer. This line of reasoning argues that the most efficient Stage 2 representation to form is one that agrees precisely with the Stage 1 representation in its presuppositions, and this is just the model (presented previously) that best accounts for the Flores d'Arcais data.

In summary, Flores d'Arcais's data can be accommodated within the present theory of comprehension if it is assumed that subjects represent their previous knowledge at Stage 2 in a way consistent with the presuppositions of the comparative sentence they are trying to verify. Although it was argued that this assumption is an eminently plausible one, more experimental work will have to be carried out to confirm this and the other assumptions of the model in full.

4.5 *Following Instructions*

The comparative has also been studied in tasks that require subjects to place an object in accordance with a description, as in 'Make it so that the red block is higher than the black block'. Although the first study of this kind was Huttenlocher's (1968) theoretical paper on deductive reasoning, this was explicitly based on her previous work on locatives and actives and passives, as described in section 3. The main thrust of the 1968 paper was to present an explanation for deductive reasoning based on the notion that people treat the propositions of a three-term series problem as an instruction to arrange objects in a series — in this case on an imaginary visual display. Huttenlocher's paper has been followed up more recently by two studies, Huttenlocher et al. (1970) and Clark and Peterson (in preparation). In order to put all this information together, however, it is necessary first to examine the properties of the comparative as a locative and to explore the consequences of those properties.

4.51 *Point of reference in comparatives*

Since the comparative sentences *A is higher than B* and *A isn't as high as B* both describe locations, they might be expected to have properties similar to the locative, and they do. For locatives we saw that there were constraints on what could be used to answer the question *Where is A?* The same constraints hold for comparatives, as can be seen in the question-answer sequences of **61**:

   61 a)   Where is A? A is higher than B.
   b)   *Where is B? A is higher than B.
   c)   Where is A? A isn't as high as B.
   d)   *Where is B? A isn't as high as B.

Like locatives, a comparative or equative construction describes where its subject is with respect to its predicate term. The term in the predicate — B in **61** — always serves as a reference point of position.

These facts can be stated in terms of presupposition. The sentences *A is higher than B* and *A isn't as high as B* both presuppose that the height of B is known, as indicated in a rough paraphrase of the former, *A is at some height that is greater than the known height of B*. It is this presupposition that accounts for the unacceptability of **61b** and **61d**, for the question *Where is B?* implies that B's position is *not* known whereas the two answers *A is higher than B* and *A isn't as high as B* presuppose that B's position *is* known. In other words, the comparative *A is higher than B* has presuppositional properties very similar to the locative *A is above B*, and since this is true, the comparative and locative should share many properties when they are used in carrying out instructions.

The point of reference is as important in the comparative as it was in the locative. Again, it is assumed that instructional tasks can be treated as implicit question-answering tasks. When the subject has A in his hand and is told 'Make it so that A is higher than B', the notion is that the subject implicitly asks 'Where should A go (or be), given that I know the position of B?', and he then tries to match this question with the instruction he was given to come up with the correct answer. So at Stage 1, the subject encodes the instruction; at Stage 2, he encodes the implicit question; at Stage 3, he compares the two representations to find the answer; and at Stage 4, he carries out the instruction.

To examine this process in more detail, imagine that the subject was holding a red block in his hand and imagine that he was looking at a display with a blue block in it. The first instruction given to the subject is 'Make it so that the red block is higher than the blue block'. This instruction and the implicit question would be represented at Stages 1 and 2, respectively as **62a** and **62b**:

   62 a)   ((red block is high +) (known (blue block is high)))
   b)   ((red block is X) (known (blue block is high)))

In this notation, I have explicitly represented the point of reference in the (*known (blue block is high*)) type of notation; furthermore, I have represented the question *Where should the red block be with respect to the blue block?* in a comparative

SEMANTICS AND COMPREHENSION

form, since this notation represents both the form the answer must be in and the information that the position of the red block is being questioned with respect to the blue block. The Stage 1 and Stage 2 representations in **62** are obviously fully congruent, so the Stage 3 comparison process would find it necessary only to replace X by $high+$, forming the implicit instruction 'The red block should be higher than the blue block'. At Stage 4, it is a simple matter for the subject to conform to this instruction by placing the red block higher than the blue block.

In contrast to this simple problem, consider the subject holding a red block and given the instruction, 'Make it so that the blue block is higher than the red block'. The Stage 1 and Stage 2 representations for this problem are shown in **63a** and **63b**, respectively:

63 a) ((blue block is high+) (known (red block is high)))
   b) ((red block is X) (known (blue block is high)))

The two strings **63a** and **63b** are now quite incompatible and require much mental manipulation before they become congruent. We can only speculate at this point on exactly what these manipulations are, but it is sufficient to assume simply that they are time-consuming operations not required by the problem represented in **62**. This analysis therefore predicts that the problem represented in **62** should be solved more quickly than the problem represented in **63**. In the same way, the instruction 'Make it so that the red block isn't as high as the blue block' is represented in **64a**, and 'Make it so that the blue block isn't as high as the red block' in **65a**; it is assumed for both instructions that the red block is in hand and the blue block is fixed, giving the implicit questions **64b** and **65b**:

64 a) ((red block is high) (known (blue block is high+)))
   b) ((red block is X) (known (blue block is high)))
65 a) ((blue block is high) (known (red block is high+)))
   b) ((red block is X) (known (blue block is high)))

Again, **64** shows congruence, and **65** does not.

The relative difficulty of instructions **62** through **65** can be summarized quite simply. In placing a red block in an array that already contains a blue block, the subject must ask himself implicitly, 'Where is the red block to go, given that I know the position of the blue block?'. Since this query contains an implicit *where*-question, it is easily answered only by those instructions that also presuppose that the position of the blue block is known. Thus, instructions **62** and **64** should be easy, and **63** and **65** should be hard.

.4.52 *Experiments on the comparative as an instruction*

The most direct study on the instructional properties of the comparative is found in Clark and Peterson (in preparation). Rather than ask subjects to place blocks in an array, as Huttenlocher and Strauss (1968) asked their very young subjects to do, Clark and Peterson gave the subject a red pencil, a black dot on a piece of paper, an instruction like 'The black dot isn't as far left as the red dot', and asked him to place a red dot in the appropriate place on the paper as quickly as he could, while he was timed. Although this experiment was successful, it was somewhat cumbersome mechanically and the timing was not very accurate. For this reason, Clark and Peterson carried out a similar experiment in which subjects were presented printed instructions like 'The blue one isn't as high as the pink one'. With a blue line off to the right of the sentence, the subject was to 'draw' in a pink line in the appropriate place with respect to the blue line by pressing one of two vertically arranged buttons; the upper button represented the drawing of a line above the blue one, and the lower button the drawing of a line below the blue one. The displays were presented in a tachistoscope, and the subject was timed from the presentation of the display to the press of the button. I will describe only the second experiment since the first one, with the black dots and red pencil, produced much the same results as the second.

The sentences Clark and Peterson used had either *the blue one* or *the pink one* as the subject, and *is higher than, is lower than, isn't as high as, isn't as low as, is better than, is worse than, isn't as good as,* or *isn't as bad as* as the relational term. For the evaluative relations, the subjects were told to think of the lines with the better one on top and the worse on the bottom; this is how subjects normally place evaluative objects in a vertical array (cf. DeSoto et al. 1965; Clark 1969a; Jones 1970).

The results of this experiment are in full agreement with the model I have described above. When subjects were asked to 'draw in' the pink line, each of the eight kinds of sentences was responded to faster when *the pink one* was in the subject position than when it was in the predicate. The occasional errors subjects made further support this conclusion. There were fewer errors when *the pink one* was in the subject position than when it was in the predicate. These results also constitute additional evidence for the principle of lexical marking, for those sentences with *high* were answered 194 msec faster than those with *low*, and those with *good*, 208 msec faster than those with *bad*.

It is instructive here, however, to contrast the results of the instructional task with those of the two-term series problems discussed above. The present claim is that the instructional task is equivalent to answering questions like those in **66**:

    66 a) If A is higher than B, then where is A? [On top]
        b) If A is higher than B, then where is B? [On bottom]
        c) If A isn't as high as B, then were is A? [On bottom]
        d) If A isn't as high as B, then where is B? [On top]

These are very similar to the two-term series problems in **67**:

    67 a) If A is higher than B, then which is higher? [A]
        b) If A is higher than B, then which is lower? [B]
        c) If A isn't as high as B, then which is higher? [B]
        d) If A isn't as high as B, then which is lower? [A]

Clearly, the comparatives, or conditionals, of **66** and **67** are identical, and it is only the information requested of the comparatives that is not. But the important congruence relation in **66** is that between the points of reference of the comparative and its question, whereas the important congruence relation in **67** is that between the underlying presupposed semantic dimensions (*height* vs. *lowness*) of the comparative and question. Considerations of congruence predict that **66a** and **66c** should be answered more quickly, respectively, than **66b** and **66d**, and **67a** and **67c** more quickly, respectively, than **67b** and **67d**. To state these predictions another way, when the conditional is a strict comparative (e.g. *A is higher than B*), it is always easier to answer questions about the subject of the sentence (A) than about B, no matter whether the question is a *where-* or *which*-type question. In contrast, when the conditional is a negative equative (e.g. *A isn't as high as B*), this is not the case: it is easier to answer *where*-type questions about the subject of the sentence (A), but easier to answer *which*-type questions about the term in the predicate (B). Following instructions, therefore, will not have the same properties as answering *Who is higher?* type questions, even though the properties for both are predictable from the principle of congruence.

4.53 *Deductive reasoning*

We now return to the deductive reasoning problems like *If John is better than Pete, and John is worse than Dick, then who is worst?* in order to examine two important attempts (DeSoto et al. 1965; Huttenlocher 1968) to explain the relative difficulty of three-term series problems. Both of these theories were founded on the premise that people reason in their mind's eye by setting up and manipulating imaginary symbols that stand for the three terms of the problem. I have included these two theories under the rubric of 'following instructions', because both of them (Huttenlocher quite explicitly) treat the comparatives of each problem as an instruction to construct an imaginary display. What is important about these two imagery theories, however, is that since they both make predictions that are different from those of the linguistic theory that I have championed above, one can use empirical results to test the validity of the theories. In fact, the available evidence appears to support the linguistic theory and invalidate the two imagery theories. But let us look more closely at both the theories and the evidence.

4.531 *Theory of spatial paralogic.* DeSoto et al. (1965) were the first to suggest that one could explain the relative difficulties of three-term series problems by appealing to a theory of 'spatial paralogic'. First, they noted that people often say that they actually do set up imaginary arrays in their mind's eye while solving these problems. Given *A is better than B*, the subject will imagine an A above a B; then given a second proposition *B is better than C*, he will imagine the full complement, with A which is above B, which is above C. When asked for *Who is best?*, the subject merely 'looks' at the top of the array, picks out *A*, and says 'A'. If this *is* what subjects actually do, DeSoto et al. pointed out, then the difficulties of the three-term series problem with *better* and/or *worse* could be explained by two principles: (1) the principle of preferred direction (my nomenclature) states that it is easier to construct or read off displays from top down than from bottom up; and (2) the principle of end-anchoring states that it is easier to construct or read off displays from the ends in than from the center out. As it happens, these two principles predict difficulty correctly for the comparative problems that DeSoto et al. examined, but not for the negative equative problems that I examined (Clark 1969a, b).

The principle of directional preference predicts that a problem like **68**:

> **68** A is better than B
> And B is better than C

should be easier than **69**:

> **69** C is worse than B
> And B is worse than A

because the subject will always build **68** from the top down and **69** from the bottom up. Subjects do, in fact, report that they visualize both problems with A on top and C on the bottom. But this principle also predicts that **70**:

> **70** A isn't as bad as B
> And B isn't as bad as C

should be easier than **71**:

> **71** C isn't as good as B
> And B isn't as good as A

for exactly the same reasons. And Jones (1970) has found that subjects generally do set up **70** and **71** with A on top and C on the bottom. However, the results of Clark (1969a), shown in Table XI, go directly counter to this prediction, with **70** actually harder than **71**. According to the principle of lexical marking, of course, this result is quite explicable, since **70** has the more difficult *bad* underlying it and **71**, the easier *good*. Thus, the principle of lexical marking succeeds where DeSoto et al.'s principle of directional preference fails.

Their second principle, end-anchoring, predicts that **72**:

> **72** A is better than B
> And C is worse than B

should be easier than **73**:

> **73** B is worse than A
> And B is better than C

since the propositions in **72** both mention the extreme terms (A and C) before they mention the middle term B, but the reverse is true in **73**. That is, the subjects construct a visual representation from the ends in in the former problem, but from the center out in the latter. However, this principle also predicts, and for exactly the same reasons, that **74**:

> **74** A isn't as bad as B
> And C isn't as good as B

should be easier than **75**:

75 B isn't as good as A

And B isn't as bad as C.

This prediction is incorrect, as the results of Clark (1969a), shown in Table XI, indicate. On the other hand, we saw that the principle of congruence correctly predicts that **74** (Problem III' in Table XI) should be harder than **75** (Problem IV'). So here again, the linguistic principle succeeds where the principle from the theory of spatial paralogic fails.

4.532 *Theory of constructing visual imagery.* Huttenlocher has proposed a theory of constructing visual imagery in order to account for many of the same phenomena that DeSoto et al.'s theory was designed to account for. The main difference between her theory and DeSoto et al.'s was that she attempted to construct a more satisfying explanation for the end-anchoring effects found by DeSoto et al. Her thesis was this: People typically show certain difficulties in following instructions that are couched in terms of comparative sentences. For example, as we saw in section 3 and earlier in this section, it is easy to place something expressed as the subject of a locative or comparative sentence, but difficult otherwise. If people construct visual images in the same way they construct actual physical arrays, the tasks that require imagery should therefore show the same difficulties as the tasks that require physical manipulation. It is important to see what predictions this theory makes.

Consider the incomplete problem in **76** (analogous to Problem III in Table XI):

76 A is better than B

And C is worse than B.

After reading the first proposition, the subject would set up a visual image with A above B. The important point in the process, however, comes in the placement of the third object C. Since B is already in place, C will be easy to place with respect to B if C is the subject of the second proposition. This conditions hold for **76**, so **76** should be a relatively easy problem to solve. In contrast, consider **77** (analogous to Problem IV in Table XI):

77 B is lower than A,

And B is higher than C.

Reading the first proposition here would result in a visual image of A above B. But in this case, the third term C, to be placed with respect to B, is in the predicate of the second proposition and should therefore be difficult to place. The theory predicts, then, that **76** should be easier than **77**, a prediction that is verified in Table XI.

But this theory makes incorrect predictions for the negative equative problems analogous to **76** and **77**. Consider **78** and **79** (Problems III' and IV', respectively, in Table XI):

78 A isn't as bad as B,

And C isn't as good as B.

79 B isn't as good as A,

And B isn't as bad as C.

78 has the same properties as **76**, since C, the third term to be placed, is the subject of the second proposition. By Huttenlocher's theory and because the subject term is easier to place in negative equatives as well as comparatives (cf. Clark and Peterson's results), **78** should be relatively easy. By contrast, **79** should be hard just as **77** was, since in **79** the third term to be placed (C) is in the predicate of the second position. But the results in Table XI show that **78** is harder than **79**, not easier, as Huttenlocher's theory predicts. Thus this demonstration (and other data in Clark 1969a, b) appears to disconfirm Huttenlocher's theory of constructing visual images.

This argument invalidating Huttenlocher's imagery theory was presented in Clark (1969a, b), but more recently, Huttenlocher, Higgins, Milligan, and Kauffman (1970) have replied to that argument, giving more evidence said to favor the theory of constructing spatial images against the invalidating argument just presented. Although there are too many details to go into here (cf. Clark and Peterson, in preparation), I would like to show briefly how this additional evidence does not save the theory of constructing spatial images from the disconfirmation just made.

The invalidation argument presented in Clark (1969a, b) required only one assumption in order to test the original Huttenlocher proposal, and that was that C would be easier to manipulate physically when it was the subject of a negative equative instruction, as in *C isn't as good as B*, than when it was in the predicate, as in *B isn't as good as C*. Although unverified at that time, that assumption, as we saw, has since been confirmed by Clark and Peterson (in preparation), so the invalidation argument of Clark (1969a, b) remains unchanged. In order to counter this argument, however, Huttenlocher et al. (1970) carried out two pairs of parallel experiments. In one experiment, for example, they had their subjects solve three-term series problems in their heads, and in the parallel experiment, they had different subjects solve the same problems visually on a felt-board, by placing felt figures with names on them in a vertical array on the board. The subjects were timed in both instances. Since the results of the two experiments were virtually identical, Huttenlocher et al. argued (1) that the subjects must have gone through the same mental operations in the first experiment as they did in the second, and (2) since the subjects were manipulating objects in the second experiment, they must have been manipulating imaginary objects in the first. Both parts of this conclusion, however, are logically invalid. One could just as easily argue in the second part, for example, that since the subjects were carrying out the linguistic processes of the linguistic theory in the first experiment, they must have been doing the same in the second. Without any additional evidence, therefore, these data could just as well support the linguistic theory as the imagery theory.

But there is additional evidence, and it shows at least that the subjects do not behave in a manner consistent with the imagery theory. The requisite evidence is that the subject of negative instructions is easier to place than the predicate, as demonstrated in Clark and Peterson (in preparation). The logic is as follows: (1) Clark and Peterson found that the surface subjects of both the comparative and the negative equative constructions are easier to place in instructional tasks than the predicate. (2) Since (1) is true, Huttenlocher's (1968) imagery theory would predict that problems like **78** should be *easier* than problems like **79**. (3) But Huttenlocher et al. and Clark (1969a, b) found for both the reasoning and the feltboard experiments that problems like **78** were *harder*, not easier, than problems like **79**. Therefore, (4) since the imagery theory makes incorrect predictions in this instance, it must be wrong. In short, the existing data run counter to Huttenlocher's particular imagery theory, yet are quite consistent with the present theory of comprehension.

4.6 *Comprehension of Comparatives by Children*

One surprising source of support for the present analysis of the comparative is to be found in the literature on comprehension in children. In several previous studies, children of various ages have been required to understand comparatives in carrying out several types of tasks. It was found that these children persisted in making several types of mistakes that revealed deficiencies in their understanding of the adjectives underlying the comparative as well as in their understanding of the comparative construction itself. The most extensive studies of these phenomena have been carried out by Donaldson (1963), Donaldson and Balfour (1968), and Donaldson and Wales (1970). Although I have discussed the relevance of these studies to adult comprehension in detail elsewhere (Clark 1969a; Clark 1970b), I will summarize the arguments briefly here.

One of the main facts to be accounted for is that children about three and one-half years old consistently misunderstand the word *less* as if it were the word *more*. Donaldson and Balfour gave their young subjects two cardboard trees with cardboard apples on them and asked them 'Which tree has more apples on it?' and 'Which tree has less apples on it?'. All of the children, except for one or so of the more sophisticated ones, pointed to the tree with more apples on it in answer to *both* questions. Similarly, Donaldson and Wales gave their subjects other graded sets of objects and asked them questions like 'Give me one that's bigger than this one', 'Give me one that's wee-er than this one', 'Point to the biggest one', and 'Point to the wee-est one' (the children, obviously, were Scottish). The findings in this type of questioning were consistent with the *more-less* results: children correctly interpreted the positive adjectives (*big, long, thick, high, tall, fat*) more often than they did the implicit negative adjectives (*wee, short, thin, low, short, thin*), and this was true when the adjectives were in both the comparative *-er* and the superlative *-est* forms. It is perhaps not too surprising that children should misinterpret just those forms that adults find more difficult to comprehend, but the more basic problem is to account for both the adult's and child's difficulties in a unified theory.

It appears that we can identify several primitive stages in the comprehension of comparatives by children. These stages are characterized by the fact that children have incomplete knowledge of the adjectives and presuppositions of the comparative. I will outline a hypothetical series of stages that are (1) consistent with the data that have been collected, yet (2) ordered from the hierarchically simplest information found in the comparative to the most complex.

4.61   The first stage

Consider Donaldson and Balfour's comparative *This tree has more apples than that one*. Although the children had the superficial appearance of correctly comprehending this sentence — they made correct choices when forced to choose the tree with more apples — there is other evidence that they did not. When Donaldson and Balfour presented two equal trees and asked their subjects 'Does one tree have more (or less) apples on it than the other?', some of the children replied with expressions like 'both of them', 'both the trees', 'that one does and that one', 'they two ones', 'each tree', and 'these two have', answers which clearly do not make sense from the adult point of view. These answers, in fact, almost seem to be answers to a question like 'Does this tree or that tree have SOME apples on it?'; the answers affirm the fact that both trees have apples on them.

This observation leads to the hypothesis that *This tree has more (or less) apples on it than that tree* is interpreted at the first stage approximately as ((*this tree has some apples*) (*that tree has some apples*)), paraphrased roughly as 'This tree has some apples on it and so does that tree'. This interpretation has two important properties. First, it contains two primitive sentences, just like the comparative, and can be developed into the full comparative at a later age. And second, the comparative adjective *more* is taken to mean 'some' or 'a quantity of', which is just the NOMINAL sense that is superordinate to, or semantically presupposed by, the adjectives *much* and *little*, which themselves underlie *more* and *less*. The first stage interpretation of the comparative, therefore, contains at least the essentials of the full interpretation: it specifies that the two compared objects are on a semantic dimension, and it specifies, although only in part, what that dimension is.

This description, however, is still not enough to account for why the children in Donaldson and Balfour's study were able to interpret *more* correctly but not *less*. Note that they were asked to choose the tree that had more (or less) apples on it. If they interpreted this to mean 'choose the tree with some apples on it' they could have chosen either tree. So we have to make the additional assumption that 'some' or 'a quantity of' is best exemplified by the tree with more apples on it. This is a reasonable assumption. 'Some' or 'a quantity of' refers to a positive amount along the quantity dimension, and the tree with more apples on it is not only an example of such a positive amount, but it is also positive in amount with respect to the other tree. The lesser amount would be taken as the reference point for the quantity dimension perceptually, as certain other studies have shown.

In all, there is a surprising amount of evidence for this primitive first stage in the acquisition of the comparative.

First, the fact that *less* is interpreted as if it meant *more*, and *shorter* as if it meant *longer, wee-er* as if it meant *bigger,* etc., is consistent with the above characterization of the first stage of acquisition. That is, since both *more* and *less* would mean 'some' or 'a quantity of', it would appear that *less* was being interpreted as *more*, just as Donaldson and Balfour found.

Second, the elliptical answers 'both of them', 'that one does and that one', and the like that Donaldson and Balfour observed constitute evidence for the proposal that the interpretation consists of two underlying propositions. As pointed out above, these answers could be considered shortened versions of, e.g. 'That one has some and that one has some', answers that quite explicitly express the two underlying propositions.

Third, Donaldson (1963) and Duthie (1963) found that some young children interpreted *Betty is older than May* to be the same as *May is older than Betty* and even as *Betty is younger than May.* For these children, apparently, the sentences were all synonymous and meant simply something like 'Betty is different in age from May'. This example again indicates that the children were simply interpreting the sentences in terms of the nominal sense ('of age') of the words *younger* and *older.* Also, the children showed that they 'knew' the two underlying sentences of the comparative by taking into account the age of both Betty and May. The one additional fact that this example shows is that *Betty is younger than May* did not mean for these children simply 'Betty is so old and May is so old'; the interpretation had the additional constraint that the ages had to be different, although it did not matter in which direction the difference lay.

Fourth, in his study of how children solved three-term series problems with quantified comparative sentences (e.g. *Tom is four years younger than Dick*), Duthie (1963) found that some of the youngest children treated the underlying adjective in its nominal sense quite explicitly. One child, for example, was asked in the middle of a problem how he knew that Tom was four; he replied, 'Because it says that Tom is four years younger than Dick' (p. 237). Other children made the same error with 'four years older' and other similar constructions. Both *younger* and *older* appear to have taken on the nominal meaning 'of age' for these children.

4.62 *The second stage*

The second stage is a transitional one in which the comparative *Betty is younger than May* is interpreted approximately as ((*Betty is young*) (*May is young*)), which can be paraphrased as 'Betty and May are young but (perhaps) different in age'. The children at this stage will have passed from the point at which they interpreted *younger* and *older* simply to mean 'of age' to the point at which they 'know' that *younger* and *older* indicate something about the age of Betty and May relative to some standard age. Although the evidence for this transitional stage is still less adequate than one would like, it can be seen in the following illustrations.

First, Piaget (1921) studied the mistakes that nine- and ten-year-olds made in solving the following three-term series problem (from Burt 1919): *Edith is fairer than Suzanne; Edith is darker than Lili. Which of the three has the darkest hair?* To quote Piaget (1928): 'It is as though [the child] reasoned as follows: Edith is fairer than Suzanne so they are both fair, and Edith is darker than Lili so they are both dark. Therefore Lili is dark, Suzanne is fair, and Edith is between the two. In other words, owing to the interplay of the relations included in the test, the child, by substituting the judgment of membership (Edith and Suzanne are "fair", etc.) for the judgment of relation (Edith is "fairer than" Suzanne), comes to a conclusion which is exactly opposite of ours.' (p. 87). Piaget's interpretation of these mistakes is consistent with the proposal that children in this transitional stage interpret *Edith is fairer than Suzanne* as ((*Edith is fair*) (*Suzanne is fair*)), a notation that specifies 'judgment of membership' without indicating 'judgment of relation'.

Second, Donaldson (1963) studied the mistakes children made in solving the problem: *Dick is shorter than Tom. Dick is taller than John. Which of these three boys is tallest?* Like Piaget, Donaldson found that some children had great difficulties putting the information from two premises together. One main problem for Donaldson's subjects, however, was that the 'judgment of membership' — the judgment that *Dick is shorter than Tom* implies simply that Dick and Tom are short — induced them to think that there were four people instead of three. Since Dick was short in the first premise, but tall in the second, and since these two facts are incompatible, many children simply assumed that there must be two Dicks, a tall one and a short one. For example, one young girl's solution to the above problem was, 'This Dick [second premise] is tallest, John is next tallest, Tom is third and then it's Dick [first premise]' (p. 131). In this example, the child could grasp the comparative information within premises, but she could not put information from the two premises together because of the disparity in the underlying adjectives. The children in Donaldson's study made the two-Dick error in all types of problems, but most often in those problems in which Dick appeared in two comparatives with different underlying adjectives (like the above problem).

Third, some of the children in Donaldson's study verbalized the underlying presuppositions of the problem directly. One child, for example, seemed to be unable to interpret comparative information one moment, but quite able to the next. This child was quoted as saying, 'It says that Dick is shorter than Tom, so Dick is short and Tom is short too'. But in the next sentence she continued, 'And Dick is taller than John so Dick is tall and John is short' (p. 131). In the first sentence the child is expressing the underlying presuppositions of the sentence, and this is consistent with the proposed representation of the comparative at this transitional second stage; in the second sentence, the child is expressing the comparative information in the only way she knows how, with the non-comparative adjectives *tall* and *short*.

It should be noted that children who are at this stage can appear to answer questions like *Which is taller?* and *Which is shorter?* correctly without a full understanding of the comparative information. Since *Which is taller?*, for example, presupposes *tallness,* and this is something that the child knows at this stage, the child can simply pick out the tall object as opposed to the short one in answer to the question; this action would be consonant with his primitive interpretation of the comparative, and would also appear to be correct. Problems of the kind Piaget referred to are required before one can see that the child has not grasped the full meaning of the comparative.

4.63 *The third stage*

In the third and final stage in the acquisition of the comparative, the child is able to appreciate the complete meaning of the comparative, treating *Betty is older than May* as ((*Betty is old*+) (*May is old*)), just as an adult would.

In the processing of comparatives by adults, examples have been given to demonstrate that subjects must manipulate the underlying presuppositions of the comparative and question into congruence before the problem can be solved. Some of Donaldson's children, in fact, made this manipulation quite explicit. One boy was given the problem: *Tom is taller than Dick. Dick is taller than John. Which of these three boys is shortest?* The boy promptly explained, 'This means Dick is shorter than Tom, John is shorter than Dick. So that gives the answer — it's John' (p. 121). To make the premises congruent with the question *Who is shortest?*, he explicitly rephrased both of the premises in terms of *shorter.* When asked why he did this, he answered, 'I thought it would help'. Donaldson reports that many other children did this too.

In summary, the acquisition literature suggests that children comprehend the comparative in much the way that adults do. The children appear to treat the comparative as an amalgam of two sentences and take into account the underlying adjectival dimension of the comparative. The difference between children and adults is that children appear to have less complete knowledge of the comparative. The youngest children, for example, appear to interpret the underlying adjective in only its 'nominal' sense, and while this sense identifies the semantic dimension on which the two compared objects are found, it does not contain any comparative information. The children who are slightly older appear to interpret the underlying adjectives contrastively (e.g. *young* vs. *old*), but this is still not enough for true comparisons. This child must be fairly old (perhaps as much as ten years old) before he is able to grasp all the subtleties of the adult interpretation of the comparative. As a note of caution, however, it must be pointed out that before these (or any other) hypothetical stages can be taken seriously, much more systematic investigation is needed of the comprehension of comparatives by children.

4.7 *Summary*

In this section, I have presented a model of how people represent the comparative (*John is better than Pete*) and equative (*John is as good as Pete*) constructions and have tried to demonstrate how these representations would be used within a general theory of comprehension to account for several phenomena in the comprehension of comparatives. The three principal properties of these representations were (1) that they contain the two objects being compared, (2) that they specify the underlying semantic dimension on which the two objects were presupposed to be compared, and (3) that they indicate that the second of these two compared objects is the presupposed point of reference. The previous results on answering questions were shown to be accounted for by assuming that the subject had to make the premise and question congruent in their presuppositions before the question could be answered. Similar constraints were required to account for the previous results on paraphrasing and sentence verification. It was in the tasks that required subjects to follow instructions that the point of reference of the comparative was important. If the point of reference of the task to be carried out was different from the point of reference described in the comparative instruction, then the instruction was difficult to follow.

A second issue discussed in this section was the relative difficulty of implicitly negative or marked comparative adjectives (e.g. *worse*) over their positive counterparts (e.g. *better*). A large number of such positive-negative pairs were discovered in the comprehension literature and were shown to fit what I have called the principle of lexical marking. Furthermore, the evidence from children's misinterpretations of comparative adjectives seems particularly strong on this point: at first children are correctly able to 'interpret' only the unmarked adjectives, and even when older, they are more likely to err on marked than unmarked adjectives.

5. ACTIVE AND PASSIVE SENTENCES

Among the earliest constructions to be studied in transformational-generative linguistics were the simple active and passive (affirmative declarative) constructions. In 1957, for example, Chomsky argued that *William likes Furness* and *Furness is liked by William* express the same underlying proposition and should therefore be derived from the same underlying source. Chomsky's proposal was that active and passive sentences are derived from identical kernel sentences; the derivation of a passive, however, requires a Passive Transformation in addition to certain obligatory transformations. Since 1957, there has been much linguistic debate on the derivation of the passive (and its corresponding active, for that matter), and the debate still continues. In this section, the goal is not to solve all the difficult linguistic problems associated with the passive, but rather to use what is known to suggest certain properties of the comprehension of actives and passives.

The active and passive constructions have also had a long history of controversy within psychology. It all started with Miller (1962) who first proposed a cognitive theory of comprehension that might now be described as follows: To understand a sentence, a person must derive the deep structure of that sentence. And to do that, he must consider the surface structure, work backwards through the transformations that would produce that surface structure from deep structure, and come up with the proper deep structure. Thus, an active sentence should take less time to comprehend than its corresponding passive, since a person can derive the deep structure of the active relatively directly, but that of the passive only by 'detransforming' the surface structure through the passive transformation. It also follows that negative passives will take more time than either negatives or passives alone, since the former require at least one more transformation than either of the latter, and so on. Miller's hypothesis eventually became known as the derivational complexity hypothesis: sentences that are derivationally more complex should be more difficult to understand than those that are less complex. The subsequent popularity of the active and passive contrast has been immense: it has been used both by those trying to confirm or disconfirm the derivational complexity hypothesis and by those who simply wanted two constructions that apparently differed in difficulty.

Since Miller's original paper, a number of studies have given support to the derivational complexity hypothesis (e.g. Miller and McKean 1964; Mehler 1963; Savin and Perchonock 1965), but just as many or perhaps more have raised questions about it. For example, if active and passive sentences are remembered in the same form except for a footnote for the passive indicating that it requires an extra transformation, the pattern of errors in memory for the deep structure subject, verb, and object of the active and passive ought to be similar; but empirically the patterns differ considerably (Anderson 1963; Coleman 1964). Another prediction of this hypothesis is that the deep propositions of the sentence are retained in memory, and the footnotes specifying how to transform them into particular surface structures are lost independently of those deep propositions; evidence to the contrary has been found by Fillenbaum (1966, 1968a, b), Sachs (1967), Clark and Clark (1968), Clark and Stafford (1969), Clark and Card (1969), and others. In comprehension, Gough (1965, 1966), and Slobin (1966), for example, have argued that the derivational complexity hypothesis cannot explain a number of the consistent differences in verification times that they found with active, passive, positive, and negative sentences. More recently, Fodor and Garrett (1966) and Watt (1970) have argued from very general evidence that the derivational complexity hypothesis just cannot be correct. For example, Watt (1970) pointed out that this hypothesis would predict *For anyone to please Dee is hard* should be easier to comprehend than *Dee is hard to please*, a prediction, like many many other similar ones, that is surely false.

The particular point that many psychologists have worried about is that active and passive sentences emphasize different things, and this seems contrary to the derivational complexity hypothesis. *Jeffrey sired Rhodri* seems to 'emphasize' Jeffrey, whereas *Rhodri was sired by Jeffrey* seems to emphasize *Rhodri* instead. The difference has been called one of 'theme' (Clark 1965; Clark and Begun 1968), 'emphasis' (Johnson-Laird 1968a, b), 'salience' or 'focus of attention' (Turner and Rommetveit 1968; Tannenbaum and Williams 1968), and so on. Although the phenomenon alluded to by these various expressions has received little attention from transformational linguists, they have in some excellent studies by Firbas (1964), Halliday (1967), and other linguists. Yet a complete psychological account of active and passive sentences and their comprehension will have to deal with this problem, particularly since it seems to take on immediate importance in many psychological tasks.

In spite of the differences between actives and passives, however, one fact remains: people will judge *Jeffrey sired Rhodri* and *Rhodri was sired by Jeffrey* to be synonymous in some sense. Later in this section, we will examine several studies that seem to show that whatever else is wrong with the derivational complexity hypothesis, it is correct in claiming that the propositions expressed by an active and its corresponding passive are the same. And this fact is in full accord with intuition. The part of the derivational complexity hypothesis that fails to hold up is the identification of comprehension difficulty with derivational complexity — with number of transformations intervening between surface and deep structure. So the analysis that is about to be offered will retain the requirement that the propositional content of actives and passives be the same, while discarding the requirement that the process of deriving deep structure be the inverse of a linguistic derivation of the comprehended sentence.

5.1   The Representation Problem

The first requirement for the representations of actives and passives, then, is that they indicate the same propositional structure. Thus, we might represent the propositional content of *Vivienne saves money* and *Money is saved by Vivienne* by **80**:

     80   (Vivienne save money)

In a more elaborate notational scheme, of course, we would want to represent the actual functional relations or cases (a la Fillmore 1968) of the three words, indicating that *Vivienne* is the agent, *money* is the object, and *save* is the verb. We might also want to indicate that *Vivienne* is the subject and *save money* is the predicate, although psychologically this will be seen to have less importance than the case relations. So it should be remembered simply that the three positions within the parentheses stand for Agent, Verb, and Object (or Recipient).

English, however, contains very few true transitive verbs, and in fact *save* is not one of them. *Vivienne saves money* is really a causative construction (Chomsky 1965; Lyons 1968) that can be paraphrased approximately as *Vivienne causes money to be safe* — that is, as an embedded sentence something like **81**:

81 (Vivienne causes (money be safe))

English causatives will always look something like **81**, with a *cause* (actually an abstract verb closely related to the word *cause*) as the embedding verb and with one or another type of embedded sentence. Sets **82** through **88** all show how the causatives in **a**, paraphrased approximately as **b**, contain the simpler sentence in **c**.

82 a) John moved the car.
   b) John caused the car to move.
   c) The car moved.
83 a) Fats killed the roach.
   b) Fats caused the roach to die.
   c) The roach died.
84 a) Tommy crated the apples.
   b) Tommy caused the apples to be in a crate.
   c) The apples were in a crate.
85 a) The Navy enlisted the men.
   b) The Navy caused the men to be on a list.
   c) The men were on a list.
86 a) Helen enlarged the hole.
   b) Helen caused the hole to be larger.
   c) The hole was larger.
87 a) Charlotte cleaned the windows.
   b) Charlotte caused the windows to be clean.
   c) The windows were clean.
88 a) Horace taught Rogers how to drive.
   b) Horace caused Rogers to learn how to drive.
   c) Rogers learned how to drive.

It is evident from these illustrations that causatives can be of many types. The embedded **c** sentences can be simple intransitives, as in **82** and **83**; locatives as in **84** and **85**; simple attributives, i.e. sentences with predicate adjectives, as in **86** and **87**; or even transitive sentences, as in **88**. Furthermore, although the causative verb is often identical or similar phonetically to its embedded intransitive verb, as with *move-move, lay-lie, set-sit*, etc., it sometimes is not, as with *kill-die* in **83** and *teach-learn* in **88**. Once all the causative verbs have been removed from the list of what appear to be transitive verbs in English, only a few 'true' transitives remain, e.g. *hit* as in *Melvin hit the ball*. But even these 'true' transitives are suspect, for they too seem to indicate an agentive or causative function of the subject; it is just that these verbs do not seem to have corresponding intransitives in English. When Fillmore (1968) calls *Melvin* in *Melvin hit the ball* Agentive, he appears to be claiming that all proper transitives have this causative function in common. But whatever the linguistic theory turns out to look like, transitive sentences (excluding those with instrumental subjects, like *The knife cut the butter*, those with receptive subjects like *John saw the fight*, and certain others) can be said to be causative in nature.

One reason for discussing the causative nature of most transitive sentences is to give us a way of talking about certain differences between active and passive sentences. Consider the sentence *Fats killed the roach*. This sentence can be divided up approximately into a cause and an effect: the cause of the roach's dying is Fats (or rather some action by Fats), and the effect of this cause was that the roach died. The sentence *Fats killed the roach*, roughly, presumes that Fats acted as the cause of something, and it asserts that the effect was that the roach died. But the corresponding passive sentence *The roach was killed by Fats* presumes approximately that something happened to the roach, and it asserts that what happened was that the roach died and furthermore that Fats was the cause of that death. In other words, the active and passive differ in what is presumed by the speaker to be known to the listener: the cause or what was affected.

All this subjective analysis can be firmed up with a few linguistic examples. Consider the question-answer sequences in **89**:

89 a) What did Fats do? Fats killed the roach.
b) What did Fats do? The roach was killed by Fats.

Clearly, **89a** is acceptable whereas **89b** without contrastive stress is not. On the other hand, the pattern is reversed for the question-answer sequences in **90**:

90 a) What happened to the roach? Fats killed the roach.
b) What happened to the roach? The roach was killed by Fats.

In this case **90b** is acceptable, whereas **90a** without contrastive stress is not. In accord with the subjective analysis, the question *What did Fats do?* presupposes that Fats effected something, whereas *What happened to the roach?* presupposes that the roach was affected by something. The simpler question *What happened?*, which presupposes only that something happened, is answered equally well by *Fats killed the roach* and by *The roach was killed by Fats,* as it should be, since the presupposition that something happened is implied by the respective presuppositions of the active and passive sentences. It should be pointed out here that *What happened to the roach?* can be answered simply by *The roach was killed* without a specification of the causative agent, even though such an agent is always implicit in the passive. The passive can always be agentless. Similarly, the full effect need not be specified in an answer to *What did Fats do?*, for the answer could be *Fats ate*, a sentence in which the object of the verb is implicit. Only a few English verbs, however, allow the deletion of the object.

The linguistic evidence just presented, then, must be taken into account in considering how people mentally represent the information in active and passive sentences. The semantic representations apparently should reflect two pieces of information: (1) that the propositions underlying the two constructions are the same; and (2) that what is asserted by the two is different. A notation that approximates these two goals for sentences **91a** and **92a** is shown in **91b** and **92b**, along with approximate paraphrases of those representations in **91c** and **92c**:

91 a) Fats killed the roach.
   b) (Fats did (Fats cause (the roach die)))
   c) As for what Fats did, he killed the roach.
92 a) The roach was killed by Fats.
   b) ((Fats cause (the roach die)) happened to the roach)
   c) As for what happened to the roach, it was killed by Fats.

Both **91b** and **92b** contain the same underlying proposition (*Fats cause (the roach die)*), but the embedding clauses of **91b** and **92b** are different: the embedding clause of **91b** is meant to indicate that what Fats did is being asserted, while that of **92b** is meant to indicate that what happened to the roach is being asserted. Moreover, the representations in **91** and **92** express the facts illustrated in **89** and **90** quite directly. They also reflect the respective pseudo-cleft sentences for **91a** and **92a** — namely, *What Fats did was kill the roach* and *What happened to the roach was that it was killed by Fats*. The particular notation conventions used in **91** and **92** should not be taken as final, but rather as a temporary means for expressing the important semantic facts that need representing. For the present, the exact form of the notation is less important than the notions the representations are meant to express.

Observations very similar to those just made can also be found in the work of Firbas (1964) and Halliday (1967). Firbas, for example, pointed out that sentences tend to open with thematic elements and close with rhematic elements, where 'thematic elements are such as convey facts known from the verbal or situational context, whereas rhematic elements are such as convey new, unknown facts'. Halliday (1967), in adopting this terminology, has spoken simply of *theme* and *rheme*, where in the active sentence the theme is usually the agent, and in the passive the theme is the object; the theme is the noun phrase presumed known from context. But this view of theme does not seem quite complete enough to express the differences required for the question-answer sequences in **89** and **90**. Under this view of theme, *Fats killed the roach* asserts something about Fats, not about what Fats did; its paraphrase would be *As for Fats, he killed the roach*, instead of *As for what Fats did, he killed the roach*. Likewise, under this view the passive would be paraphrased as *As for the roach, it was killed by Fats*, instead of as the more complete *As for what happened to the roach, it was killed by Fats*. Even though theme does not seem complete enough for present purposes, the word 'theme' will nevertheless be a convenient term to use in referring to the surface subjects of the active and passive sentences and to their presuppositional effects.

With the suggestive representations of **91** and **92** in mind, we can now proceed to the psychological literature on active and passive sentences. In the sections that follow, I will take up the topics of semantic judgments — that is, what people understand the active and passive sentences to mean — sentence verification, and question answering, followed by a discussion of certain universals of word order in transitive sentences.

5.2 *Semantic Judgments*

One method for studying how people understand or represent active and passive sentences is to ask people what such sentences mean. Rather than ask subjects this question directly, however, the psychologist would normally ask subjects to make a comparative judgment of some sort — how similar are these two sentences in meaning? how sensible is this sentence? which of these two situations is better described by this sentence? which of these two sentences is more acceptable? and so on. Some of these methods are designed to bring out the gross similarities between two different constructions, and others, their subtle differences. So it should be kept in mind that all the studies to be examined do not reveal every facet of meaning in active and passive sentences.

5.21 *Judgments of similarity and anomaly*

The gross similarity between actives and passives is nicely demonstrated in a study of Clifton and Odom (1966). Their interest, among others, was to measure the judged similarity between pairs of constructions all derived from the same underlying proposition — in particular, the simple active, simple passive, negative, question, negative passive, passive question, negative question, and passive negative question. The subject was given a proposition in one syntactic form — e.g. *The house was not built by the carpenter* — and was asked to judge its 'similarity' to the same proposition in all the other seven syntactic forms.

The predictions the present analysis makes of these results are based on the two separate aspects of the representations: first, their identical underlying propositions, and second, their differing embedding strings. First, actives and their corresponding passives should be judged highly similar, since they contain the same underlying propositions. Actives and passives should be more similar, for example, than actives and their corresponding negatives, or passives and their corresponding negatives, since in these latter cases, subjects will rightly judge a proposition and its denial to be quite dissimilar in meaning. Clifton and Odom's data confirm these predictions: simple actives and passives were judged more similar than any other pair of constructions in their study.

The second type of prediction is derived from the differences between actives and passives. Note, for example, that the active question *Did Melvin strike Eloise?* asks for confirmation of what Melvin did, not of what happened to Eloise, while the reverse is true of the passive question *Was Eloise struck by Melvin?* That is, the yes/no questions corresponding to actives and passives do not query the underlying propositions themselves, but rather the strings in which they are embedded — i.e. (*Melvin did* ()) and (() *happened to Eloise*), respectively. The active and passive questions might therefore be paraphrased as **93** and **94**:

93 As for what Melvin did, did he strike Eloise?

94 As for what happened to Eloise, was she struck by Melvin?

The representations of **93** and **94** would be more congruent with positive statements of the same voice rather than the opposite voice, since active statements assert what active questions ask about, and passive statements assert what passive questions ask about. In short, active and passive questions should be judged more similar to simple affirmatives in the same voice than in the opposite voice. This prediction is verified in Clifton and Odom's results. The analogous predictions, based on parallel arguments, can be made to show that actives and passives should be more similar to negative statements in the same voice, that active and passive questions should be more similar to negative statements in the same voice, and so on. All these predictions are upheld in Clifton and Odom's data.

A second study on judgments of semantic anomaly (Clark and Begun 1968) supports the present analysis in quite a different way. In that study, subjects were asked to judge on a scale of 1 to 7 how sensible or nonsensical certain sentences were. The sentences were constructed by taking perfectly good active sentences and substituting words from other random sentences into them as the agent, verb, or object, or sometimes in both the agent and verb position, and so on; the substituted word or words, however, were always of the same form class as the word they replaced. The resulting sentences, which ranged from very sensible to very nonsensical, were judged by the subjects in both their active and passive forms. If the judged 'sensibleness' of the active and passive sentences is merely a judgment of the sensibleness of their underlying propositions, as we should expect, then an anomalous active and its passive counterpart should be judged equally anomalous regardless of voice. The results confirmed this prediction: judgments of anomaly were made of the underlying proposition and were not affected by voice.

But a second part of the Clark and Begun study was more revealing. Consider *The calf lassoed the president* and *The president was lassoed by the calf*, two sentences containing the same underlying proposition and judged equally nonsensical. In a second part of the study, subjects were asked simply to change one word (a noun or verb) in each sentence to make the sentence more sensible. Given the first sentence, subjects were most likely to change *lasso* or *president*, but not *calf*, whereas given the second sentence, they were most likely to change *lasso* or *calf*, but not *president*. So even though both sentences were judged as equally nonsensical, subjects saw the anomaly as arising out of different sources: the deep verb or object contained the anomaly in the first sentence, but the deep verb or agent contained the anomaly in the second. Apparently, the subjects accepted the presuppositions that the calf had done something in the active and that something had happened to the president in the passive; they accepted the themes of the two sentences as given or known. As a consequence, they saw the anomaly arising out of what the calf had done and in what had happened to the president, respectively, and were loath to alter the themes. These results, then, further support the two properties of active and passive representations — their common underlying propositions, and their differing embedding propositions or themes.

5.22 *Judgments of 'emphasis' in active and passive sentences*

Slightly less direct evidence for the proposed representations of active and passive sentences is to be found in two studies by Johnson-Laird (1968a, b). His hypothesis was simply that active sentences lay emphasis on the agent in the underlying proposition, whereas passives lay emphasis on the object. In terms of the representations in **91** and **92**, the noun mentioned in the embedding sentence — the theme of each sentence — is the one that is 'emphasized' in both sentences.

In one study, Johnson-Laird gave his subjects two sentences — say, *Red follows blue* and *Blue is followed by red* —, two long rectangles on a piece of paper, and a red and a blue crayon. The subjects were instructed to color in parts of the rectangles corresponding to the agent and object of each sentence in such a way that another person could figure out which of the two sentences referred to which of the two rectangles. The results were just as Johnson-Laird expected. The subjects tended to make the color of the surface subject (the theme) cover more of the rectangular strip than the color of the remaining term; and this effect was more pronounced for passives than for actives. In a second study, Johnson-Laird gave his subjects symmetrical or asymmetrical diagrams of the same kind and asked them to judge the relative appropriateness of several active and passive sentences for those diagrams. The results in this study confirmed the conclusions drawn for the first. In short, subjects tend to emphasize the theme — the term presupposed to be known — in both actives and passives.

5.23 *Definiteness of the theme in active and passive sentences*

In agreement with Firbas (1964) and Halliday (1967), the present analysis has assumed that the theme or surface subject of an active or passive sentence is normally presupposed by the speaker to be known to the listener. This assumption has several immediate implications. First, the theme should normally be a definite noun phrase — e.g. *the roach* as opposed to *a roach* —, since definite noun phrases require or presuppose previous mention of their referents, whereas indefinite noun phrases imply that their referents are being introduced for the first time. Second, the theme should often be expressed as a pronoun, since pronouns are shorthand for previously mentioned or situationally implied nouns. Third, the theme should be brief, since the theme, as a noun phrase already known to the listener, normally requires few if any qualifying relative clauses or adjectives. These three predictions are nicely demonstrated in Svartvik's (1966) statistical examination of an extensive corpus of English prose. He found that the theme in passives was most often definite, contained about half as many words on the average as the agent, was a pronoun far more often than the agent was, and so on. Although Svartvik did not collect the comparable statistics on the active, it seems likely that the theme of the active (normally the agent) would have comparable properties.

Consider definiteness alone in a proposition like *baker watched candlestick-*

maker. If only one of the noun phrases is definite, it will normally be made the theme of the sentence. So when *baker* is definite and *candlestick-maker* is indefinite, **95a** will seem appropriate, and **95b**, though possibly acceptable, will certainly seem inappropriate:

95 a) The baker watched a candlestick-maker.

 b) A candlestick-maker was watched by the baker.

But when *candlestick-maker* is definite and *baker* is indefinite, the reverse will be true, with **96b** more appropriate:

96 a) A baker watched the candlestick-maker.

 b) The candlestick-maker was watched by a baker.

The inappropriateness of **95b** and **96a** seems even more pronounced when the sentences of **95** and **96** are preceded by contexts that mention the definite noun phrase and truly motivate its definiteness, or when the definite noun phrases in each sentence are replaced by the pronoun *he*. Thus, whichever of the agent or object is definite will normally be made the theme, since it is the noun phrase that is presupposed known from previous context.

5.24 *The interpretation of quantifiers in active and passive sentences*

Closely related to the properties of definiteness just discussed are certain properties of indefinite determiners as investigated in a very interesting pair of studies on quantifiers by Johnson-Laird (1969a, b). These studies were apparently based on Chomsky's (1957) observation that '*Everyone in the room knows at least two languages* may be true, while the corresponding passive *At least two languages are known by everyone in the room* is false' (p. 101). In particular, Johnson-Laird noted that in **97**,

97 a) Every philosopher has read some books.

 b) Every book has been read by some philosopher.

the *some* is normally taken to mean 'some or other', whereas in **98**,

98 a) Some books have been read by every philosopher.

 b) Some philosopher has read every book.

the *some* is normally taken to mean 'some in particular'. Whether *some* is interpreted as 'some in particular' or as 'some in general' depends, as Johnson-Laird noted, not on its function in the underlying proposition, but rather on whether it is the theme of the sentence or not. To give these informal observations more empirical backing, Johnson-Laird devised a technique by which subjects could indicate non-linguistically what they understood sentences like **97** and **98** to mean. This experiment supported his informal observations as well as several subsidiary predictions that need not concern us here. In a second study, Johnson-Laird asked other subjects to decide whether inferences like the following were true or false: *Every philosopher has read some books; therefore, some books have been read by every philosopher.* Since *some or other* logically implies *some in particular*, but *some in particular* does NOT imply *some or other*, the inference '**97a** therefore

98a' will normally be judged as true, whereas the inference '**98a** therefore **97a'** will be judged as false. In sum, Johnson-Laird demonstrated with normative data that *some* is usually interpreted as 'some in particular' when it is the theme of an active or passive sentence, but as 'some or other' when it occurs as the object of the active or the agent of the passive.

The property Johnson-Laird has investigated in quantifiers is what Fillmore (1967b) has called 'specificity'. Indefinite determiners, according to Fillmore, can be marked as either +Specific ('some in particular') or —Specific ('some or other'). One particular place where this feature is necessary is in sentence negation. Consider *Some philosopher has read every book.* Whenever *some* is marked as +Specific, then to indicate that it is false that some PARTICULAR philosopher has read every book one would have to say *Some philosopher hasn't read every book.* But whenever *some* is marked as —Specific, then to indicate that it is false that some philosopher OR OTHER has read every book one would have to say *No philosopher has read every book.* Thus, the feature ±Specific has concrete syntactic consequences besides the obvious differences.

One very important consequence not discussed by Fillmore is that —Specific quantifiers cannot be antecedents for definite pronouns in subsequent clauses. Consider the sentences in **99**:

> **99 a)** *Every philosopher has read some books, but they aren't very exciting books at all.
>
> **b)** Every philosopher has read Plato's *Republic* and Aristotle's *Poetics*, but they aren't very exciting books at all.
>
> **c)** Some books have been read by every philosopher, but they aren't very exciting books at all.

Note that **99a**, in which the *some* is normally interpreted as —Specific, is decidedly odd; the *they* in the second clause seems to have no well-defined antecedent. The *they* is not wrong because it refers to a noun phrase in the predicate of the sentence, for **99b** is perfectly acceptable; and it is not wrong because it refers to an indefinite noun phrase, for **99c** is acceptable too. The difference between **99a** and **99c** is that the former contains a —Specific *some*, while the latter contains a +Specific *some*. The definite pronoun *they* must apparently have a +Specific antecedent. This is further demonstrated in **99d** and **99e**:

> **99 d)** *Few books have been read by every philosopher, but they aren't very exciting books at all.
>
> **e)** A few books have been read by every philosopher, but they aren't very exciting books at all.

As Fillmore pointed out, *few* and *a few* are respectively —Specific and +Specific, no matter where they occur. If —Specific quantifiers cannot be antecedents to definite pronouns, then **99d** should be odd, but **99e** acceptable, and this agrees with our judgments of the acceptability of these sentences.

These facts about specificity in the antecedents to definite pronouns enable us to account for Johnson-Laird's results if we assume the semantic representations of actives and passives given earlier. Consider the paraphrases for the semantic representations of **97a** and **98a**, respectively:

100 a) As for what every philosopher has done, he has read some books.

b) As for what has happened to some books, they have been read by every philosopher.

100a contains nothing to force anything other than a —Specific interpretation on *some books*, whereas **100b** does. Since *some books* in **100b** is the antecedent for the definite pronoun *they, some books* must be +Specific. These interpretations of **100a** and **100b** are in agreement with facts that Johnson-Laird has pointed out. Although the paraphrases in **100** are probably not completely accurate reflections of the underlying semantic representations of **97a** and **98a**, they do demonstrate two points: (1) the surface subject of a sentence introduces a theme, and for the rest of the sentence to refer back to this theme, it must be a well-defined object; (2) therefore, if the theme is indefinite, it must be marked as +Specific, for otherwise no definite statement can be made about it. Apparently, indefinite noun phrases are normally assumed to be non-specific; it is only when the indefinite noun phrases must be +Specific for thematic or other syntactic reasons that the indefinite will be marked as +Specific. This informal rule, then, would account for why *some* is interpreted as +Specific in the surface subject position, but not necessarily so when in other positions.

This explanation, however, leaves two facts unaccounted for. First, people do not invariably interpret *some* in the surface subject position as +Specific (cf. Johnson-Laird's results). The reason for this appears to be that people can change the theme of a sentence by non-normal stress patterns. For example, the *some* in *Some books have been read by every philosopher* is normally taken to be +Specific, but when *books* is given contrastive stress, the *some* becomes —Specific. In the stressed version, *some books* is no longer what is 'given', so it can be taken as —Specific. The second fact to be accounted for is why the *few* in *Few books have been read by every philosopher* can still be —Specific although it is the theme of the sentence. This appears to contradict the generalization that themes must be +Specific. But it should be remembered that *few* is a negative (cf. section 2), and it appears that negation itself makes *few* —Specific. Consider the ordinary negative *John isn't at home.* While its positive counterpart *John is at home* is quite specific about John's whereabouts, the negative sentence is non-specific. The same observation can be made of *few*. The proper paraphrase of *Few books have been read by every philosopher* is probably something like *As for what has happened to books, few of them have been read by every philosopher.* In this case, *them* refers to specific books, and *few* simply denies that the number of books is many. Put another way, *few* is not part of the presupposed theme: it is part of the assertion of the sentence and, as such, it does not need to be +Specific. This is in agreement with the facts about *few* and *a few* discussed in section 2.

In summary, themes must be +Specific, and the semantic representations proposed for the present analysis in some sense 'predict' this fact. It is this property (that themes must be +Specific) that causes *some* in the subject position to be normally interpreted as 'some in particular'. It also accounts for Chomsky's observation that *At least two languages are known by everyone in the room* and its active counterpart are not synonymous, since the indefinite *at least two languages* in the passive version is the theme and must be +Specific, whereas in the active version it is not the theme and is normally interpreted as —Specific. This analysis can also be extended to account for the greater acceptability of definite over indefinite themes: definite themes are automatically +Specific and so are always acceptable, whereas indefinite themes will only be acceptable when they are interpreted as +Specific. The broader generalization appears to be that themes are more acceptable the more exactly they refer to some identifiable object; +Definite themes fit this criterion better than —Definite themes, and +Specific better than —Specific. The present semantic representations for actives and passives encompass these facts quite naturally.

5.3   Sentence Verification

In this section, I turn to two studies directly concerned with the underlying processes of comprehension in active and passive sentences. In both Gough (1965, 1966) and Slobin (1966), subjects were required to listen to a sentence, view a picture, and then judge as quickly as possible whether the sentence was true or false of the picture. As usual, these verification tasks can be divided into four stages: a sentence encoding stage, a picture encoding stage, a comparison stage in which the sentence and picture representations are compared, and a response stage. And verification latencies can be predicted from a full specification of these four stages. Unfortunately, without more data than are found in these two studies, it is impossible to specify these stages as completely as necessary. So I will present two alternative ways of viewing the process, Scheme I and Scheme II, both of which are consistent with the data of Gough and Slobin. More evidence will be required to choose between the two or to reject these two for a third.

To understand Scheme I, consider Gough's (1965) task in which the subject is presented, say, either *The boy hit the girl* or *The girl was hit by the boy* along with a picture of a boy or girl either hitting or kicking a boy or a girl. At Stage 1, it is assumed that *The boy hit the girl* is represented as (*the boy did (the boy hit the girl)*), and *The girl was hit by the boy* as ((*the boy hit the girl) happened to the girl*). At Stage 2, it is assumed that the subject sets up an active-like representation of the picture — one containing (*someone did ()*) — when he has just read an active sentence and a passive-like one — one containing (() *happened to someone*) — when he has just read a passive. In other words, the subject knows that he must encode the picture with respect to an agent in the former case, but with respect to the recipient of the action in the latter. So, for example, the picture for a true active sentence would be (*the boy did* (*the boy hit the girl*)), and that for a true passive would be ((*the boy hit the girl*) *happened to the girl*). At Stage 3, the subject would compare the representations of the sentence and picture, and at Stage 4, he would respond appropriately.

The Stage 3 comparison operations in Scheme I would be relatively simple and almost identical to the first operations of the 'true' method of negation discussed in section 2. The first comparison operation would check for the identity of the embedded strings. For true sentences, there would always be a match, and for false sentences, there would always be a mismatch. For false sentences, it is necessary to have a second operation that would change the presupposed value of the truth index *true* to a new value of *false*. Since this second operation would consume time, the false sentences would take longer than the true ones.

Gough's (1965, 1966) latencies can be applied to Scheme I. They are easily summarized: actives took less time than passives; true sentences took less time than false ones; and these two effects were independent of each other. The second result — that true sentences should be faster than false ones — follows directly from Scheme I, but the first result is not so obvious. To explain the active and passive difference, it must be assumed that (1) actives take less time to represent at Stage 1 than passives; or (2) pictures take less time to represent in an active format than in a passive format; or (3) both (1) and (2) are the case. A second study of Gough's (1966) eliminates the first possibility. Whereas in the first study the picture was presented simultaneously with the first consonant of the last word of the sentence, in the second study it was presented 3 sec. after the initial consonant of the last word. In the first study, then, it might perhaps be assumed that the representation of the sentence was still being constructed after the picture had been presented; but this is highly implausible in the second study. Nevertheless, actives took less time than passives in both studies — 90 msec in the first and 115 msec in the second. So the active-passive difference in Gough's tasks cannot be accounted for by differences in representation time (although his results do not preclude such a difference, since he measured latencies from the end of each sentence rather than the beginning). In conclusion, Scheme I would have to attribute the active-passive difference to the relative difficulty of representing pictures in a passive-format.

Now consider Scheme II. It does not differ from Scheme I at Stage 1. But at Stage 2, it is assumed that the picture is invariably represented in an active-format — for example, as (*the boy did* (*the boy hit the girl*)). Stage 3 must therefore contain an additional set of comparison operations. The first operation, say, compares the embedding strings of the sentence and picture representations. For active sentences, of course, this operation will find a match. But for passives, it will find that (() *happened to the girl*) and (*the boy did* ()) are not identical, so a second operation will manipulate, say, the second string to make it identical to the first, in this case by changing (*the boy did* ()) into a passive format (() *happened to the girl*). The third and fourth operations would repeat the comparisons of Scheme I, checking the identity of the embedded strings and changing the truth value just in case there is a mismatch. As for latencies, the second operation would be applied only in the case of passive sentences, making passives take longer than actives; and the fourth operation would apply in the case of false sentences, making false take more time than true. Thus, Scheme II would also accurately predict the latencies of Gough's first two studies; but in Scheme II, passives would take longer than actives because of an extra Stage 3 operation.

In their essentials, however, Schemes I and II both attribute the increased diffi-culty of passives to the same thing: the picture must be represented in a passive format before it can be compared to the representation of a passive sentence, and representing the picture in this way takes more time. Some possible reasons for this difference will be taken up in section 5.5.

5.31 *Encoding strategies*

The study by Slobin (1966) contains an important innovation over Gough's studies of active and passive sentences. Slobin distinguished what he called re-versible sentences from non-reversible ones. *The boy hit the girl* — one of Gough's sentences — is reversible since the sentence still makes sense with the agent and object interchanged — e.g. *The girl hit the boy* —; but *The girl picked the flower* is non-reversible, since *The flower picked the girl* is anomalous. Slobin's basic finding was that whereas actives were faster than passives when they were reversi-ble, there was no difference between actives and passives when they were non-reversible. Slobin suggested that this was perhaps due to the fact that the agent and object in the non-reversible sentences can be distinguished semantically and need no help from the syntax, hence both active and passive sentences are equally easy to comprehend. But if we take this suggestion to mean that the Stage 1 encoding of non-reversible actives and passives is now equivalent, this still does not explain why Gough found active-passive differences in his 3-sec. delay condition.

Slobin's important result, however, might be accounted for in the picture en-coding stage. The pictures for reversible sentences will always contain two animate objects — boys or girls, for example, in Gough's tasks. Since this is the case, the subject cannot discriminate agent from recipient in the pictures without judging what the action is and which of the two people instigated the action. By this process alone, the picture could well be coded in an active format more quickly than in a passive format. But the picture for reversible sentences will always con-tain one animate and one inanimate object, and so the subject can immediately discriminate agent from recipient. Thus, if the sentence is active, he can imme-diately code the picture in terms of what the agent did, and if the sentence is pas-sive, he can immediately code what happened to the recipient of the action. To account for Slobin's results the two codes in this case would have to take the same amount of time to construct.

Note that this explanation favors Scheme I over Scheme II. That is, the source of the active-passive difficulty in Gough's tasks and in Slobin's reversible sentences derives from the fact that a picture is more easily coded in an active format, by first perceiving the instigator of the action and then encoding what he did. In the case of non-reversible sentences, the normal process of encoding the picture can be bypassed, since the instigator and recipient of the action are both readily perceived and the correct coding can be made relatively quickly in either case.

5.4 Answering Questions

The psychological literature contains several excellent examples of question-answering tasks for active and passive sentences. All these examples appear to support the present proposals for the semantic representations of active and passive sentences.

5.41 The Wright study

The main study to be considered is Wright's (1969), which contains some of the most convincing evidence available that is counter to Miller's (1962) original thesis that actives and passives are simply represented in the identical form (except for the footnote specifying voice). Briefly, Wright read her subjects 60 sentences one at a time; 5 sec. after each sentence, she asked the subjects a question about that sentence. Half the sentences were active, and half were passive, and half the questions were active, and half were passive. The questions asked for the agent, the object, or the verb by various means — e.g. *Who followed the girl? By whom was the boy followed? What did the boy do?* etc. Her interest was in the number of errors subjects made on each type of question. Indeed, it is somewhat of a surprise that subjects should make any errors at all on this task, but Wright found errors in about 13% of the answers. And as she expected, subjects made more errors in answer to some questions than to others. But before we examine these errors, it is profitable to see just what the present theory would predict.

Let us consider the schematic active and passive sentences *A hit B* and *B was hit by A* and the possible questions that could be asked of them. These two sentences would be represented at Stage 1 as **101** and **102**, respectively:

> **101** (A did (A hit B))
> **102** ((A hit B) happened to B)

The first two active questions to be considered, *Who hit B?* and *Whom did A hit?*, would be represented at Stage 2 by **103** and **104**, respectively:

> **103** (X did (X hit B))
> **104** (A did (A hit X))

The two passive questions *By whom was B hit?* and *Who was hit by A?* are given in **105** and **106**:

105 ((X hit B) happened to B)

106 ((A hit X) happened to X)

For purposes of the Stage 3 comparison process, it is obvious that the active questions **103** and **104** are congruent with **101**, but incongruent with **102**, whereas the passive questions **105** and **106** are congruent with **102**, but incongruent with **101**. So the first prediction is that a question in the same voice as the sentence should be easier to answer than one in a different voice, since in the latter incongruent cases, the representations of the sentence and question must be manipulated in some (unknown) way to make them congruent.

But this simple principle — that same voice is easy and different voice is hard — will not work for questions asked of the verb. The two active questions *What did A do?* and *What happened to B?* can be represented as in **107** and **108**:

107 (A did (X))

108 ((X) happened to B)

The two passive questions *What was done by A?* and *What was done to B?* are perhaps best represented as **109** and **110**:

109 (A did (X))

110 ((X) happened to B)

Representations **107** and **109** were made identical since it is difficult to differentiate what is asked for in *What did A do?* and *What was done by A?*; the second question, for example, does not seem to imply that there was necessarily a recipient of the action (as the normal passive would imply), and both questions are answered acceptably by the simple sentence *He ran.* The questions *What happened to B?* and *What was done to B?*, on the other hand, both necessarily imply a recipient of an action and so are represented in the same way, as **108** and **110**, even though the first question allows a broader range of answers — e.g. *He died, He fell,* etc. — which do not contain agents. Although there is some uncertainty about representations **107** through **110**, they seem to be approximately correct.

The representations in **107** through **110**, however, are either directly congruent or directly incongruent with the sentence representations in **101** and **102**: **107** and **109** are congruent with **101**, the active sentence, and **108** and **110** are congruent with **102**, the passive sentence. The Stage 3 process of replacing the X by the appropriate subcomponent in the sentence representations should therefore be easy in the congruent cases, but difficult in the incongruent ones.

Wright's (1969) results are shown in Table XIV. The sentence-question sequence is given on the left, and the correct answer and percentage of errors for each sequence are shown on the right. (Wright, obviously, used a large variety of full English sentences; *A hit B* is simply a schematic example.) Her data confirm all the predictions made above, and in considerable detail. First, when the voice of the sentence and question were alike in the *who* questions, subjects made few

TABLE XIV. *Percentage errors from Wright (1969)*

Sentence	Question	Correct Answer	Errors
A hit B.	Who hit B?	A	3%
A hit B.	Whom did A hit?	B	6
A hit B.	By whom was B hit?	A	3
A hit B.	Who was hit by A?	B	19
B was hit by A.	Who hit B?	A	6
B was hit by A.	Whom did A hit?	B	6
B was hit by A.	By whom was B hit?	A	1
B was hit by A.	Who was hit by A?	B	7
A hit B.	What did A do?	hit B	7
A hit B.	What happened to B?	hit by A	17
A hit B.	What was done by A?	hit B	8
A hit B.	What was done to B?	hit by A	10
B was hit by A.	What did A do?	hit B	14
B was hit by A.	What happened to B?	hit by A	9
B was hit by A.	What was done by A?	hit B	16
B was hit by A.	What was done to B?	hit by A	7

errors; otherwise they made many. To illustrate, the active questions *Who hit B?* and *Whom did A hit?* each elicited fewer errors from *A hit B* than from *B was hit by A*, whereas the reverse was true for each of the passive questions *By whom was B hit?* and *Who was hit by A?* Second, voice made no difference in the *what* questions (at the bottom of Table XIV), just as predicted; nevertheless, congruence of underlying representations did. Thus, *What did A do?* and *What was done by A?*, both of which presuppose that A caused something and ask for an effect, were easier for *A hit B*, which presupposes that A caused something and asserts what that effect was. In contrast, *What happened to B?* and *What was done to B?*, both of which presuppose that B was affected by something and ask what the effect and cause were, were easier for *B was hit by A*, which makes the same presupposition and asserts what is asked for. In short, the principle of congruence predicts the main differences in these data quite nicely.

Wright's data show several other striking effects. Perhaps the most obvious one is that subjects were able to answer with the agent more accurately than with the (deep structure) object, and this effect is quite independent of the voice of the sentence and question. This generalization, of course, cannot be made without reference to the propositions that underlie the active and passive; because of this requirement, the correct representations for actives and passives must specify these propositions in the identical form. The present proposal conforms to this require- ment, since (*A hit B*) underlies both the active and passive. Although there is no ready explanation for the agent-object difference at present, it must ultimately be accounted for by the Stage 3 comparison operations. For example, Stage 3 might first contrive to make the (*A did* ()) and (() *happened to B*) embedding strings of the sentence and question congruent, followed by the next strings in, strings of the form (*A caused* ()), followed by the most embedded strings, like (*B received a blow*) or however the innermost string would be represented. In this scheme, the agent would be processed sooner than the object, producing the desired result. Without further data, however, such a Stage 3 process is merely speculative. It should also be noted here that a simpler answer will not do. In the *what* questions, asked of the verbs, it was no easier, overall, to express what the agent did than what happened to the object, so it is not simply that the agent and what he did is 'foremost' in the subject's mind with respect to the object and what happened to it. The explanation of the agent-object effect will have to be closely tied to the form of the questions.

A second striking result of Wright's experiments is that actives are no easier than passives in a task of this type. If anything, Wright's data show that passives are slightly easier. Most previous studies have shown that actives are easier than pas- sives, but it appears, from the vantage point of Wright's experiment, that the pre- vious studies have given unfair advantage to the active. Gough's tasks (1965; 1966), for example, made it difficult to differentiate the agent from the recipient in the pictures; since humans were used as both agent and recipient, agentiveness was perhaps prominent, giving advantage to the active. In Slobin (1966), this problem was eliminated in non-reversible sentences, and passives were just as easy as ac- tives. It is important to note that Wright's sentences were reversible, and yet she still found that passives were no harder than actives. This fact reinforces the pre- vious suggestion that the difficulty of the passive over the active voice in reversible sentences comes not at the sentence encoding stage in Gough's and Slobin's experi- ments, but rather at the picture encoding stage. One could conclude that actives and passives each have their own important place in language, and when the proper conditions prevail, actives are easier than passives, or passives are easier than ac- tives. It is just that actives are probably appropriate in a wider range or more common set of contexts.

5.42 *Transitives and locatives*

In section 2 we examined two studies on answering questions of active and pas- sive sentences — namely, Smith and McMahon's (1970) and Huttenlocher's (1968) studies. Although the transitive sentences of these studies were analyzed as if they contained implicit locatives, they could also be viewed as true actives and passives. What is important is that the locative and transitive analyses of these sentences yield the same predictions and conclusions. It is worthwhile to examine these sentences as transitives and to compare this analysis with the previous locative analysis.

As usual, *A is leading B* and *B is led by A* (as two examples) will be represented at Stage 1 by **111** and **112**, respectively:

    111   (A did (A lead B))

    112   ((A lead B) happened to B)

The problem is how to represent the questions *Who is ahead?* and *Who is behind?* so that they could ever be made congruent with **111** and **112**. The most obvious solution is simply to treat them as actual transitives comparable to *Who is leading?* and *Who is following?* That is, *Who is ahead?* and *Who is behind?* would be represented something like **113** and **114**, respectively:

    113   (X did (X lead y))

    114   (X did (X follow y))

The words *lead* and *follow* should not be taken literally in **113** and **114**; they are rather surface representations of the notion of transitivity combined with the meanings of *ahead* and *behind*, respectively.

Once this notation has been adopted, the congruence of sentence and question becomes obvious. Let us examine the four possible premise-question sequences. First, question **113** is completely congruent with premise **111**, so the sequence **111** + **113** should be the easiest one to answer. Second, question **113** is not congruent with **112** in the embedding strings, so to answer sequence **112** + **113**, the subject would first have to change premise **112** from ((*A lead B*) *happened to B*) to (*A did* (*A lead B*)), or perform some other equivalent alteration. This second sequence should therefore be harder than the first. Question **114** is congruent with neither **111** nor **112**. So third, to answer the sequence **111** + **114**, the subject must simply change around premise **111** from (*A did* (*A lead B*)) to (*B did* (*B follow A*)), or something equivalent. And fourth, to answer the sequence **112** + **114**, the subject must change the premise even more radically; for example, he might change **112** from ((*A lead B*) *happened to B*) to (*A did* (*A lead B*)) to (*B did* (*B follow A*)), or something equivalent. That is, congruence is achieved only after a double transformation. In sum, the first sequence should be easiest, the second and third of moderate difficulty, and the fourth the hardest. This analysis implies (1) that actives should take less time than passives, and (2) that *Who is ahead?* should take less time to answer than *Who is behind?* for premises with *lead* and *precede*, but more time to answer for premises with *trail* and *follow*. In agreement with this analysis, both of these predictions are consistent with Smith and McMahon's and Huttenlocher's data.

To summarize, the transitive analysis makes the same predictions in these sentences as the previous locative analysis. And indeed it should, for these two analyses are virtually identical. The main point of contact between the two is with the basic assumption that the transitive (*A lead B*) and the locative (*A ahead of B*) are closely related. The locative analysis assumes that the latter underlies the former, while the transitive analysis assumes that the latter can be treated as if it were the former. There is good evidence, besides that presented previously, that transitives and locatives are related in just this way. Consider such pairs of sentences as: *A is across B* and *A crosses B*; *A is around B* and *A surrounds B*; *A is on top of B* and *A tops B*; etc. Such examples show that the agent of the transitive is normally equivalent to the first term of the locative, and the recipient to the point of reference of the locative. The assumption that locatives and transitives correspond in this way seems well justified.

5.5 The Universality of the SO Order

In his discussion of universals in word order, Greenberg (1963) has pointed out that the functional subject — the agent — normally precedes the object in surface structure in all the languages of his diverse sample. Although the verb might come before, between or after the subject and object, the order of the latter — S and O — is always the same. But why? The answer, as I will argue in this section, lies in how people comprehend and produce active and passive sentences and in how they perceive the world about them.

Word order is forced on language because of the way people speak. People cannot utter words in a two or three dimensional array: the array must be one dimensional. As a phenomenon intimately related to production, then, word order should reflect the constraints placed on language merely because one thing has to be expressed before another. I will consider two simple constraints placed on word order by our perceptual surroundings, and then show how these constraints could be marshalled to explain why the SO order is the normal one in all languages.

5.51 Surface structure and chronological order

The first constraint placed on language is that events must normally be expressed in chronological order whenever the chronology is not explicitly marked in another way. Consider a speaker who is describing events as they occur. By necessity, he must describe the events in chronological order, since the events being described are by definition occurring in chronological order. But this property of present tense or simultaneous descriptions appears to be the basis for the rule that all sequences of sentences in the same tense are taken to mean that the events are being described in chronological order unless otherwise marked. Consider, for example, the sequence in **115**:

   115 Melvin dropped the ball. Melvin ran across the field.

This sequence would normally be interpreted to mean that Melvin dropped the ball before, not after, he ran. And this constraint also explains why *and* is not interpreted simply as a symmetrical ampersand when it conjoins two verbs — as it normally is when it conjoins two noun phrases. In these instances, it takes on the meaning 'and subsequently' (cf. Johnson-Laird 1967; 1969c; Staal 1968) as in **116**:

116 Melvin dropped the ball and ran across the field.

And it is not that this constraint applies to adult speech alone. Children first describe events around them as well as imaginary or past events in simple sentences in perceived chronological order (E. Clark 1969). Sentence order is often the only way very young children have of indicating temporal order, for their speech lacks conjunctions and temporal adverbs, and at first it even lacks tense. Furthermore, children up to the age of about four take clause order to be the only indicant of temporal order. For example, they interpret ALL the sentences *She danced before she sang, Before she danced she sang, She danced after she sang*, and *After she danced she sang* to mean that the dancing occurred before the singing, in spite of the fact that the second and third sentences are marked to the contrary (E. Clark 1971). Since chronological order of sentences is therefore of primary importance to the interpretation of sequential events, it is likely that the following two properties of English are universal: (1) the order of two otherwise unmarked sentences in surface structure will normally be taken to be the chronological order of the events they describe; and (2) the conjunction *and* will normally take on the meaning 'and subsequently' — never 'and previously' — when it conjoins two clauses otherwise unmarked for time sequence.

5.52 Surface structure and cause and effect

The second constraint placed on language is derived from the fact that cause and effect always occur in that order — cause before effect. This is no place to discuss just when two temporally related events are also interpreted as causally related, but certain such sequences are. In these cases, two ordered sentences (again otherwise unmarked for sequence) or two sentences conjoined by *and* take on not only the meaning 'and subsequently', but also the meaning 'and consequently' (cf. Staal 1968). Note the difference between **117** and **118**:

117 a) John fell off his bicycle. He broke his arm.

    b) John fell off his bicycle and broke his arm.

118 a) John broke his arm. He fell off his bicycle.

    b) John broke his arm and fell off his bicycle.

The interpretation of **117** would normally be that the fall caused the break, but that of **118** would not. English, of course, has other ways of expressing cause and effect, as in *John broke his arm because he fell off the bicycle*, but in these constructions the cause and effect are always explicitly marked by a word like *because, since, so, consequently*, etc. Thus, since cause and effect by definition always occur in this order, the following are probably also linguistic universals: (1) the order of two otherwise unmarked clauses will normally be taken to indicate cause and effect in those cases where a causal interpretation is possible; and (2) the word *and* conjoining two such clauses will be interpreted as 'and consequently', never as 'because'.

5.53 *SO order in transitive sentences*

Now consider the cause and effect sequences in **119**:

119 a) Fats acted. The roach died.

    b) Fats acted and (as a consequence) the roach died.

Interpreted as cause-effect sequences, **119a** and **119b** are equivalent to the simple transitive sentence in **120**:

120 Fats killed the roach.

In other words, **120** is roughly an amalgamation of the two simple intransitive sentences in **119a** in a cause-effect relationship. As pointed out above, the sequence of primitive sentences in **119a** has one single property that distinguishes it as a cause and effect sequence, and that is the surface structure order of the two primitive sentences *Fats acted* and *The roach died*. The most natural way to amalgamate these two sentences, then, would be to preserve this order while making other alterations. The most primitive way to amalgamate, of course, is simply to conjoin the two sentences, as in **119b**. More complete amalgamations, however, are shown in **121**:

121 a) Fats' actions caused the roach to die.

    b) Fats' actions made the roach die.

    c) Fats caused the roach to die.

Sentences **121a** and **121b** still contain the two primitive sentences *Fats acted* and *The roach died* in quite explicit form; sentence **121c** drops explicit mention of Fats' actions, but retains explicit mention of the roach dying; finally sentence **120** amalgamates *cause to die* in a single verb *kill*. In going from **119** through **121** to **120**, one is going from the most productive to the least productive expression of cause and effect; that is, any cause and effect sequence can be expressed as in **119**, but the possibilities are vastly limited when one is forced to choose a transitive construction as in **120**. The most important fact about this series of amalgamations, however, is that the one distinctive property of **119** — the surface order of the cause and effect — is preserved through the series. In the final amalgam **120**, the order of the cause (what Fats did) and the effect (what happened to the roach) is preserved in the subject-object order. It is natural that all languages should likewise evolve a special transitive construction that preserves this cause-effect order. And this, of course, would account for why Greenberg found that the SO order is universal as the normal, unmarked order of the subject and object in transitive sentences.

The universality of the SO order can be viewed in a different, but equivalent way. In perceiving cause-effect sequences, people will normally view the causing event before the caused event — because that is by definition the order in which they occur. Thus, a simultaneous description of these events should mention the cause before the effect. Just as the surface order of two otherwise unmarked sentences reflects the chronological order of the two events described by them, so should the mention of the causative agent before the recipient of the action reflect the chronological order in which the agent and recipient are perceived. This implies again that the SO order is the *normal* order, whereas the OS order, as in the passive, should be marked, or non-normal.

It is interesting to note that a number of other facts about English transitive sentences might also be derived from the temporal properties of cause and effect. This argument, again, depends on the close relationship of time and space spoken of in section 3. Note that *from here to there* implies a direction of movement, from the source *here* to the goal *there*. Likewise, movement is also implied in temporal descriptions as in *from noon to midnight*, which is always taken to mean the time interval with noon as its beginning not as its end. That is, the *from*-phrase indicates the preceding time and the *to*-phrase, the following time. Now notice the prepositions that are often used in transitive sentences. First, there is the *to* in *Melvin kissed Eloise and he also did it to Irene.* The *to* in the second clause is merely to indicate that Irene is the recipient of the action — the goal or the end-point in the cause-effect sequence. Second, there is the *out of* and *from* in *Julia left out of anger* (meaning *Anger caused Julia to leave*) and *Constance was in great pain from the accident* (meaning *The accident hurt Constance greatly*). The *out of* and *from* in these examples indicate the causal agent, the beginning of the cause-effect sequence. (For many other illustrations of *to* and *from* underlying transitive sentences, see Gruber 1965.) These examples of *to* and *from* underlying transitive sentences in English are quite consistent with the view that *to* and *from* reflect the chronology of the cause and effect sequence underlying transitives.

We are now in a position to say why it should be easier to encode a picture in an active format than a passive format (cf. section 5.3). People normally perceive a cause and effect sequence in its natural chronological order. So a plausible way to encode a picture that is alleged to show a cause and effect relation is first to start at the beginning, finding the causal agent and encoding what he did, rather than to start at the end, finding the recipient of the action and asking what happened to him. The former strategy, of course, results in a representation of the picture in an active format. For non-reversible sentences (like *Margaret picked the flower*), however, the recipient can be determined in the picture without identifying the action at all, so the picture can be encoded with respect to what happened to the recipient. This might well be the reason why actives and passives do not differ for non-reversible sentences, but do for reversible sentences.

On the one hand, E. Clark (1969, 1971) has shown that children rely heavily on order in surface structure as an indicator of chronological order; and Clark and Clark (1968) have shown that even adults are strongly affected by clause order in memory tasks. In another context Bever (1970) has argued that a primary strategy for both children and adults is to try always to interpret a noun-verb-noun sequence first as agent-verb-object, unless there is some indication to the contrary. One of Bever's pieces of evidence for this strategy is that children at certain ages consistently interpret passives like *The cow was kissed by the horse* to mean *The cow kissed the horse*, while they rarely do the reverse. But if transitive sentences are viewed as an implicit conjunction of cause and effect, and in that order, then Bever's strategy, if correct, appears to be just a special case of the more general strategy E. Clark (1971) has noted — namely, that children first take surface order to be identical to chronological order. That is, children interpret noun-verb-noun sequences as agent-action-object, not as object-action-agent, simply because the agent and object are in chronological order in the former sequence, but not the latter. Of course, this explanation is confounded with frequency of occurrence in English, since actives with agent-action-object order are more common than passives. But one could argue that actives are more prevalent than passives for just this reason: it is only the actives that are in agreement with the universal SO order that is demanded by the two surface order constraints discussed previously.

In sum, it is not at all implausible that certain facts about actives and passives can be accounted for ultimately by two very general (and probably universal) constraints on word order. First, a sequence of unmarked sentences is taken as describing its constituent events in chronological order. Second, such chronological sequences can further be interpreted under the appropriate circumstances as cause and effect. One consequence of these two constraints is that the cause should universally be described before the effect in normal surface order, thus accounting for the universality of the SO order in languages of the world. Furthermore, these two constraints give some account for the strategies children use in interpreting sequences of sentences (or clauses) and transitive sentences. This line of reasoning is just one example of how certain general properties of cognition might be thought to affect linguistic structure — here specifically surface structure — in a significant way.

5.6 Conclusion

In section 5, it has been argued that the comprehension of active and passive sentences can also be viewed as a four stage process, with the principle of congruence as the guiding rule for the comparison stage. The active and passive sentences *Fats killed the roach* and *The roach was killed by Fats*, it was seen, have the proposition (*Fats caused (the roach die)*) in common, but the active asserts what Fats did and the passive, what happened to the roach. The full representations of the active and passive were therefore given as (*Fats did (Fats caused (the roach die))*) and ((*Fats caused (the roach die)*) *happened to the roach*), respectively, in an attempt to represent both the similarities and differences between the active and passive sentences in the same format.

In a review of the psychological literature, we saw that people interpret sentences in a way that is consistent with these representations. Although actives and passives are judged as similar in meaning, the themes of the two sentences are more often treated as known, given emphasis, and interpreted as definite or specific. Next, we saw that the comprehension of actives and passives was also consistent with these representations. In verification tasks, actives were generally easier than passives. The most plausible reason for the difficulty of the passives, it was argued, is that the verifying pictures — particularly for non-reversible sentences — are easier to encode in an active rather than passive format. It was in a question-answering task that the proposed representations of actives and passives received their best support. Here we saw that active and passive questions were most easily answered when what was queried were active and passive sentences, respectively. The exception to this generalization came in questions that asked about the verb; in this case, questions asking about what the agent did were easier for actives than for passives, whereas questions asking about what happened to the object were easier for passives than for actives. So the experimental literature supports the proposal that actives and passives express the same proposition, but assert different things about it.

6. CONCLUSIONS

In section 1 of this chapter, I outlined a general theory of comprehension which suggested that people represent the meaning of a sentence in an abstract symbolic form at Stage 1, represent other information in the same format at Stage 2, compare these two representations by a series of match and manipulation operations at Stage 3, and 'convert' the symbolic Stage 3 outcome into a response at Stage 4. The most basic assumptions of the theory were (1) that sentences are represented at Stage 1 in a format similar to their linguistic deep structures, and (2) that the Stage 3 comparison process must carry out its operations in conformity with the principle of congruence. In sections 2 through 5, I examined empirical evidence on the comprehension of negatives, locatives, comparatives, and actives and passives, and demonstrated how the theory could account for the main findings on latencies and errors in the psychological data.

In this section, I will attempt to evaluate a few of the successes and failures of this endeavor. On the plus side, the most obvious success is that the theory can account for the results of previous studies. Less obvious, however, is the fact that the theory contains important empirical generalizations about the structure of 'comprehension' tasks and about the semantic coding of all types of information. These generalizations will be discussed in section 6.1. On the minus side, the theory as presented fails to cover certain points, some of which are irrelevant to the validity of this theory, others of which are more serious. These will be discussed in section 6.2. In the final section, section 6.3, I will suggest several directions the study of comprehension might take in the future.

6.1 *Two Empirical Generalizations*

6.11 *Analysis of 'comprehension' tasks*

The 'comprehension' tasks examined in this chapter have been of several different types — sentence verification, answering questions, following instructions, and paraphrasing, to mention only the most prominent. The heuristic that has been used to tie all of these tasks together is the four-stage schema, by which each task was decomposed into two representation stages, a comparison stage, and a response stage. In spite of its simple and innocent appearance, this heuristic embodies several significant empirical claims about such 'comprehension' tasks. One claim is that a sentence is represented at Stage 1 in the same way for all types of tasks. This generalization is consistent with the fact that the results from a whole gamut of tasks containing a particular construction are accounted for by the use of a single Stage 1 semantic representation. Another claim is that the Stage 3 comparison operations are guided by the principle of congruence in all types of tasks. This claim was verified by the consistent finding that 'comprehension' tasks were carried out more quickly and with fewer errors when the Stage 1 and 2 semantic representations were congruent than when they were not. Yet another claim is that reading an instruction and then following it is conceptually equivalent to reading an instruction, asking an implicit question about the instruction, answering the question, and then producing an appropriate answer. This claim also was consistent with the results of the relevant studies. Indeed, the main claims of the present theory of comprehension would not have been testable without the four-stage schema.

6.12 *The semantic representation of information*

One generalization made possible by this four-stage schema is that information encoded at Stage 2 is represented in the same format as the semantic representation at Stage 1 regardless of where that information came from. Included among the types of information encoded at Stage 2 were: pictures, previous knowledge retrieved from memory, other sentences (in verification tasks), questions (in question-answering tasks), and the physical situation (in instruction-following tasks). The evidence for this generalization was that a number of results could not have been accounted for without it. Consider the 'true' model of negation. When applied to verification tasks in which pictures, previous knowledge, and other sentences were variously used as verifying evidence, the model accounted equally well for each type of evidence. Without the generalization that all three types of evidence are coded in the same way, it would have been necessary to construct three different, but partly overlapping models of negation, ruling out the 'true' model of negation in its general form. This is clearly an undesirable consequence, and the assumption that all Stage 2 representations are semantic in form is a natural solution to this problem.

It is important to point out that other generalizations could have been possible. Whereas the Stage 1 and 2 representations were assumed to be 'semantic' or 'interpretive' in the present theory, they could have been pictorial or acoustic in form instead. Thus, it is possible to imagine a theory of comprehension in which the sentence is stored in memory acoustically, and other information is first converted into an acoustic image and compared piece by piece with the image of the sentence. For most tasks, however, alternatives like this can be ruled out as implausible a priori. When a subject is asked to decide, for example, whether *Star is above plus* is true or false of a picture of a star (*) above a plus (+), he is really being asked whether his 'interpretation' of the sentence is equivalent in meaning to his 'interpretation' of the picture. He could answer 'no' on a number of grounds: e.g. he might think that *star* cannot be used to refer to the asterisk, that the picture is upside down, or even that the sentence means 'the star is above the surface of the paper on which the plus is printed'. Clearly, it is the meaning of both sentence *and* picture that counts. So it is natural that the comparison process should operate on the comparable 'interpretations' of sentence and picture, as it does in the present theory. This generalization is discussed more fully in Clark and Chase (1972), where it is further supported by empirical evidence.

6.2 *Problems to be Solved*

The present theory of comprehension, as proposed here, contains a number of theoretical gaps. Some of these gaps are deliberate and relatively unimportant to the validity of the present theory, while others reflect fundamental questions.

6.21 *Deliberate omissions*

6.211 *The derivation of semantic representations.* Some psychologists might argue that the theory I have presented is not a theory of 'comprehension' at all, but rather a theory of 'sentence verification', 'deductive reasoning', or the like. They would point out that this theory does not specify the process many people would call 'comprehension' — i.e. the process by which people 'derive' semantic representations from the words and phrases of surface structure. Obviously, I have not attempted to account for this part of the comprehension process, nor have I intended to. One strength of the present theory is that it can stand without a specification of the process by which the semantic representations are derived. The present theory begins with the hypothetical semantic representation of a sentence, and the only assumption required is that such a representation can be derived from surface structure. How it is derived affects no part of the theory as presently stated.

The process of how people derive semantic representations from surface structure, though extremely important, is very difficult to study — witness a number of current attempts to experiment on this aspect of comprehension. More significantly, however, the present theory could be of considerable help to these current theories. The argument is as follows: Before one can develop a theory of deriving semantic representations from surface structure, one must be able to specify in some detail just what the semantic representations should look like. The latter question is most easily answered by studying how sentences behave in tasks of the kind reviewed in the present chapter. That is, the present theory specifies the form the semantic representations of sentences take in working memory, and if correct, the form of these representations should then place powerful constraints on processes alleged to derive them from surface structure. Indeed, the present theory appears to conform quite well to several current proposals about how semantic representations are derived from surface structure, proposals too extensive to review here (cf. e.g. Watt 1970; Bever 1970).

As to the charge that the present theory is one of 'deductive reasoning' rather than 'comprehension', it matters very little how one refers to the theory. 'Comprehension' is an ambiguous term: it can refer either to the process of comprehension — as in *Pierre's comprehension of English is slow* — or to the end product of comprehension — as in *Pierre's comprehension of English is poor*. Although this chapter is also about 'deduction' in the most general sense of that word, the basic concern of the chapter is with 'comprehension' in the latter sense.

6.212 *The derivation of stage 2 representations.* Another topic deliberately ignored was the theory of how people derive Stage 2 semantic representations from pictures, previous information, or the physical context of the task. Like the process of deriving Stage 1 representations, the process of deriving Stage 2 representations does not have to be specified for the present theory to be valid. Here again, one could argue that the most efficient strategy for studying this derivation process is to learn as much as possible about the end product of this process — the Stage 2 representations — and then work backwards to see what operations could derive such a representation from the pictures, previous knowledge, or the like. The present theory, if correct, puts constraints on the form such derivational processes may take.

This is not to say that there are no important problems to be solved with regard to the derivation process. Consider a priori information, like the oddness and evenness of numbers. The Wason (1961) experiments could be accounted for, it was argued, if it was assumed that his subjects encoded the information about numbers, e.g. *Eight is even*, at Stage 2 in a positive form. It seems reasonable that information of this sort should be represented in a positive form, since in more general examples it would take many negative propositions to specify the information of a single positive proposition. But it seems highly unlikely that Wason's subjects had stored intact propositions like *Eight is even* in permanent memory. This information might have been stored, for example, as a rule: if the number is a multiple of two, it is even, and otherwise it is odd. The retrieval of *Eight is even* is therefore almost certainly a derivative process, even though the evidence seems to show that the final representation of this information is in the form of the semantic representation underlying *Eight is even*. In more complex cases — e.g. Flores d'Arcais's sentence *Lions are more ferocious than sheep* —, the problem of what is stored and how it is retrieved for representation at Stage 2 is compounded; the evidence required for verification seems even more derivative here than in Wason's task. The problem of how 'interpreted' information is stored in and retrieved from permanent memory, it appears, is much farther from solution than the problems covered in the present chapter. And it will not be solved without extensive, careful empirical investigations.

6.213 *The semantic representations of lexical items*. Another problem bypassed in the present theory is the question of how most lexical items are represented. In a few instances, specific proposals were made about the representations of words — for example, in the feature notations for *above* and *below* and unmarked and marked comparative adjectives (e.g. *better* and *worse*), and in the 'propositional' decomposition of *absent*. In most instances, however, such a detailed specification was not required. It did not matter, for instance, how *star* and *plus* were represented in the Chase and Clark experiments as long as their Stage 1 representation times were independent of the remaining latencies, as was found. The representations of most lexical items are still too difficult to specify, and they add little to the main processes discussed in the present theory.

There are, nevertheless, important exceptions to this last statement. The discussion of the comprehension of sentences like *John is absent* gives just a hint of how important the representation of a single lexical item can be. That *absent* can be decomposed into *not* and *present* suggests that many other lexical items are actually a complex amalgam of primitive propositions, each embedded within another in a very specific structure. As I will suggest below, one extension of the present theory will be to study the semantic representations of such lexical items in much greater detail.

6.22 *Problems of central interest*

In the present theory, there are also several fundamental issues that are more central to its validity. Although some of these have been hinted at before, I will discuss each of them in more detail here.

6.221 *The semantic representations of sentences*. In this chapter, I have made use of a particular format to specify the semantic representations of the sentences. In an important sense, this notation is central to the theory, for it reflects the properties the semantic representations are claimed to have. For the most part, however, the function of the notation has been more to suggest what these properties are than to specify them exactly, and this has added a certain amount of imprecision to the present chapter. Although unfortunate, the imprecision seems unavoidable at the present time. Part of the problem lies in the dependence of this notation on linguistics. Few linguists have tried to specify, for example, how single lexical items like *absent* ought to be represented in a 'propositional' notation (although cf. McCawley 1968). Even less is known about how presuppositions should be represented in such a notation (cf. Fillmore 1970). Unfortunately, this chapter was heavily concerned at times both with the internal structure of lexical items and with presuppositions. Therefore, before the sometimes makeshift notational schemes of the present chapter can be improved, we will have to know much more about (1) the linguistic deep structures of these constructions, and (2) the way these structures relate to other parts of the theory of comprehension.

Closely tied to the notational problem is the question of how much of the deep structure of a sentence a person truly represents. In section 1, it was pointed out that the deep structure assumption should probably be taken in a 'weak' sense. People do not represent all the potential deep structure of a sentence each time they comprehend it, but what they do represent is consistent with deep structure. But what do incomplete or impoverished semantic representations look like? The claim is that they are 'consistent' with linguistic representations, where 'consistent' means informally that the inferences a subject will draw from his understanding of a sentence are ones that would have been drawn from a complete linguistic representation. This requirement, if correct, implies that some possible representations are 'consistent' and some are not, yet the properties of the representations specified by this requirement have not been examined so far. Another related question is: How is it possible to discover what is and what is not represented of a sentence in a particular instance? The present theory should be helpful in making decisions about this point (cf. Clark 1969a: 396 for such an example) unless the semantic representations change wildly from instance to instance. The answers to both questions, though quite out of reach at the present time, are critical to a complete understanding of the process of comprehension.

6.222 *Stage 3 comparison operations.* Throughout this chapter, the Stage 3 comparison operations have been formulated subject to several constraints. The main constraints were (1) that Stage 3 consist of an algorithmic series of mental operations, (2) that the operations symbolically compare and manipulate the Stage 1 and 2 representations, and (3) that the overall processes conform to the principle of congruence — that two representations had to be identical for a decision to be made. Stage 3 was used for making predictions of latencies; generally, the greater the number of Stage 3 mental operations required, the longer the task took. Although this series of constraints enabled us to predict the direction of most differences in comprehension time, there are only a few instances — e.g. the Clark and Chase study — for which a model has been worked out in any detail. For many other cases, plausible models were constructed, leaving most particulars of Stage 3 unspecified. To be complete the theory will have to specify the Stage 3 operations for all tasks.

At first glance, there seem to be several slight disparities among the specific models of comprehension that have been presented. First, consider the order of the comparison operations in the Clark and Chase model. Evidence indicated that the first comparison made in the Stage 1 and 2 strings was of the *embedded* strings, and this was followed by a comparison of the *embedding* strings. The order of these comparisons might be called 'inside-out'. In contrast, one of the models proposed for actives and passives contained the order 'outside-in'. Is this a significant disparity? Should the order of comparisons be the same for all types of constructions? If the answer to the last question were yes, we could add a powerful constraint to the theory of comprehension. But there are many other significant ways of constraining the order of comparison; for example, presuppositions might always be compared before assertions, or more specific information might always be compared before less specific information, and so on. The problem seems insoluble with the present paucity of data. A second disparity among the separate models of comprehension is that the Stage 3 manipulations were viewed as altering the Stage 1 representation in some cases, but the Stage 2 representation in others. Is this disparity a critical one? This question too is unanswerable at the present time.

These disparities bring us to an important issue concerning Stage 3, and that is how to build more constraints into the comparison operations. Accurate predictions about specific latencies will not be possible without constraints on the order of the comparison operations, on the possible manipulation operations, and the like. These constraints will have to be discovered empirically.

6.3 *The Future of Comprehension Theory*

Despite its problems, the present theory of comprehension holds considerable promise for future studies in semantics. Two directions in which the theory ought to be extended are towards the study of single lexical items and towards the study of more complex constructions unexplored by psychologists.

How the present theory can be utilized to study single lexical items is best illustrated by a recent study, by Carole Offir and myself, on the presuppositional properties of the words *come* and *go*. Consider the sentence *John thought, 'Mary has just come into the kitchen'*, one of the sentences we studied. One presupposition of this sentence is that John must be in the kitchen. The same sentence with *go* in place of *come* has just the opposite presupposition: John cannot be in the kitchen. (These presuppositions are spelled out in detail by Fillmore 1967a). The question is whether these two presuppositions are represented in approximately this form when one 'understands' and represents the sentence. If this were so, then the semantic representations of the sentence with *come* should 'contain' **122**, and that of the sentence with *go* should 'contain' **123**:

    122 a) John is in the kitchen.
       b) (John in kitchen)

142   HERBERT H. CLARK

123 a) John isn't in the kitchen.
  b) (false (John in kitchen))

If these presuppositions are treated in comprehension exactly as if they were assertions, then problems like *John thought, 'Mary has just come into the kitchen', therefore, John isn't in the kitchen* should be verified as follows. At Stage 1, the subject sets up the presupposition (along with the rest of the representation) (*John in kitchen*); at Stage 2, he sets up the conclusion (*false (John in kitchen)*); at Stage 3, he compares the two representations by the 'true' method of negation; and at Stage 4, he responds 'false'. With respect to this type of conclusion, the sentence with *come* is a positive, and the sentence with *go* is a negative. One could imagine, of course, other ways of representing (or deducing) the presuppositions of *come* and *go*, although admittedly the model just presented is the simplest and most appealing. The important point is, however, that the present theory of comprehension — in this case, the 'true' model of negation — is capable of testing which of these alternatives is correct. Although the *come-go* study superficially has the same appearance as any other investigation of comprehension in sentences, it is basically a study of the semantics of *come* and *go* as lexical items. As this example shows, however, the presuppositions (and more generally, the meanings) of *come* and *go* cannot be studied without placing the two words in sentential contexts. The presuppositions of *come* and *go* must be stated relative to their agentive and locative cases and relative to the speaker and listener of the utterance: none of these functional 'arguments' is specified for *come* and *go* in isolation. The same lesson can be extended to most, if not all, lexical items.

One does not have to look very far to find other examples of lexical items that can be investigated by the present techniques. In section 2, it was argued empirically that *absent* was decomposable into *not* and *present* — that is, *John is absent* can be represented as (*true (suppose (false (John is present))))*. A similar argument was applied to the quantifiers *few, scarcely any*, and their ilk, to the prepositions *out of, from*, and their ilk, and in other sections to verbs (e.g. *lead* and *follow*), subordinate conjunctions (*before* and *after*), and other lexical items. In principle, the present theory could be applied to words in any lexical category — even to nouns. In short, the present theory holds much promise for the study of single lexical items — especially those which, like *come* and *go*, have a very complicated set of underlying propositions.

The present theory can easily be extended to new construction types as well. Potential candidates include: relative clauses (e.g. *The man who hit John was struck by Dick*), complement structures (*John refused to go home*), coordinate constructions (*John neither tripped nor fell*), subordinate constructions (*John fell because he tripped*), indirect questions (*John asked Mary to leave the room*), commands (*Raise your hand*), questions (*Who left the house early?*), polite requests (*Will you please raise your hand?*), and so on. A study of these constructions should help us define the form semantic representations take in memory and the properties intrinsic to the Stage 3 comparison process, as well as many other issues raised in this chapter. But this future work seems particularly important, for it could well hold a key that both psychologists and linguists could use to unlock the secrets of language.

REFERENCES

ANDERSON, B. 1963. The short-term retention of active and passive sentences. Unpublished doctoral dissertation, Johns Hopkins University.
ANDERSON, J. 1971. The grammar of case: Towards a localist theory. London, Cambridge University Press.
AUDLEY, R. J., and C. P. WALLIS. 1964. Response instructions and the speed of relative judgments. I. Some experiments on brightness discrimination. BrJ-Psych 55.59–73.
BEM, S. L. 1970. The role of comprehension in children's problem solving. Dev-Psych 2.351–58.
BEVER, T. G. 1970. The cognitive basis for linguistic structures. Cognition and the development of language, ed. by J. R. Hayes. New York, Wiley.
BIERWISCH, M. 1967. Some semantic universals of German adjectivals. FL 3.1–36.
BURT, C. 1919. The development of reasoning in school children. Journal of Experimental Pedagogy 5.68–77, 121–27.
CAMPBELL, R. N., and R. J. WALES. 1969. Comparative structures in English. JL 5.215–51.
CHASE, W. G., and H. H. CLARK. 1971. Semantics in the perception of verticality. BrJPsych 62.311–26.
——. 1972. Mental operations in the comparison of sentences and pictures. Cognition in learning and memory, ed. by L. Gregg. New York, Wiley.
CHOMSKY, N. 1957. Syntactic structures. The Hague, Mouton.
——. 1965. Aspects of the theory of syntax. Cambridge, Mass., M.I.T. Press.
CLARK, E. V. 1969. Language acquisition: The child's spontaneous description of events in time. Unpublished doctoral dissertation. Department of Linguistics, University of Edinburgh.
——. 1971. On the acquisition of the meaning of 'before' and 'after'. JVLVB 10.266–75.
CLARK, H. H. 1965. Some structural properties of simple active and passive sentences. JVLVB 4.365–70.
——. 1969a. Linguistic processes in deductive reasoning. PsychRev 76.387–404.
——. 1969b. The influence of language in solving three-term series problems. JExPsych 82.205–15.
——. 1970a. Comprehending comparatives. Advances in psycholinguistics, ed. by G. Flores d'Arcais and W. J. M. Levelt. Amsterdam, North Holland Press.

——. 1970b. The primitive nature of children's relational concepts. Cognition and the development of language, ed. by J. R. Hayes. New York, Wiley.

CLARK, H. H., and J. S. BEGUN. 1968. The use of syntax in understanding sentences. BrJPsych 59.219–29.

CLARK, H. H., and S. K. CARD. 1969. Role of semantics in remembering comparative sentences. JExPsych 82.545–53.

CLARK, H. H., and W. G. CHASE. 1972. On the process of comparing sentences against pictures.

——. 1974. Perceptual coding strategies in the formation and verification of descriptions. Memory and Cognition 2.101–11.

CLARK, H. H., and E. V. CLARK. 1968. Semantic distinctions and memory for complex sentences. QJEP 20.129–38.

CLARK, H. H., and C. OFFIR. Forthcoming. On 'coming' and 'going'.

CLARK, H. H., and T. PETERSON. Forthcoming. Comprehension of the comparative as an instruction.

CLARK, H. H., and R. A. STAFFORD. 1969. Memory for semantic features in the verb. JExPsych 80.326–34.

CLARK, H. H., and O. YOUNG. Forthcoming. Explicit and implicit negation and its comprehension.

CLIFTON, C., Jr., and P. ODOM. 1966. Similarity relations among certain English sentence constructions. Psychological Monographs 80 (5, Whole No. 613).

COLEMAN, E. B. 1964. The comprehensibility of several grammatical transformations. Journal of Applied Psychology 48.186–90.

DESOTO, C., M. LONDON, and S. HANDEL. 1965. Social reasoning and spatial paralogic. Journal of Personality and Social Psychology 2.513–21.

DOHERTY, P., and A. SCHWARTZ. 1967. The syntax of the compared adjective in English. Lg 43.903–36.

DONALDSON, M. 1963. A study of children's thinking. London, Tavistock.

DONALDSON, M., and G. BALFOUR. 1968. Less is more: A study of language comprehension in children. BrJPsych 59.461–71.

DONALDSON, M., and R. J. WALES. 1970. On the acquisition of some relational terms. Cognition and the development of language, ed. by J. R. Hayes. New York, Wiley.

DUTHIE, J. 1963. A further study of overlap error in three-term series problems. A study of children's thinking, ed. by M. Donaldson. London, Tavistock.

EIFERMANN, R. R. 1961. Negation: A linguistic variable. Acta Psychologica 18.258–73.

FILLENBAUM, S. 1966. Memory for gist: Some relevant variables. L&S 9.217–27.

——. 1968a. Sentence similarity determined by a semantic relation: Learning of 'converses'. Proceedings of the 76th annual convention of the American Psychological Association 3.9–10.

——. 1968b. Recall for answers to 'conducive' questions. L&S 11.46–53.

FILLMORE, C. J. 1967a. Deictic categories in the semantics of 'come'. FL 3.219–27.
——. 1967b. The syntax of English preverbs. Glossa 1.91–125.
——. 1968. The case for case. Universals in linguistic theory, ed. by E. Bach and R. T. Harms. New York, Holt, Rinehart and Winston.
——. 1970. Types of lexical information. Studies in syntax. FL supplementary series, vol. 10, ed. by F. Kiefer. Dordrecht, Reidel.
FIRBAS, J. 1964. From comparative word-order studies. Brno studies in English. [Opera universitatis brunensis 93]. 4.111–26.
FLORES D'ARCAIS, G. B. 1966. On handling comparative sentences. Unpublished manuscript. Harvard University, Center for Cognitive Studies.
FODOR, J., and M. GARRETT. 1966. Some reflections on competence and performance. Psycholinguistics papers, the proceedings of the 1966 Edinburgh Conference, ed. by J. Lyons and R. J. Wales, pp. 135–53. Edinburgh University Press.
GOUGH, P. B. 1965. Grammatical transformations and speed of understanding. JVLVB 5.107–11.
——. 1966. The verification of sentences: The effects of delay of evidence and sentence length. JVLVB 5.492–6.
GREENBERG, J. H. 1963. Some universals of grammar with particular reference to order of meaningful elements. Universals of language, ed. by J. H. Greenberg, pp. 58–90. Cambridge, Mass., M.I.T. Press.
GREENE, J. M. 1970a. Syntactic form and semantic function. QJEP 22.14–27.
——. 1970b. The semantic function of negatives and passives. BrJPsych 61.17–22.
GRUBER, J. S. 1965. Studies in lexical relations. Unpublished doctoral dissertation, M.I.T.
HALLIDAY, M. A. K. 1967. Notes on transitivity and theme in English: II. JL 3.199–244.
HANDEL, S., C. DeSOTO, and M. LONDON. 1968. Reasoning and spatial representation. JVLVB 7.351–7.
HORN, L. R. 1969. A presuppositional analysis of 'only' and 'even'. Papers from the Fifth Regional Meeting, Chicago Linguistic Society, pp. 98–107.
HUDDLESTON, R. D. 1967. More on the English comparative. JL 3.91–102.
HUNTER, I. M. L. 1957. The solving of three-term series problems. BrJPsych 48.286–98.
HUTTENLOCHER, J. 1968. Constructing spatial images: A strategy in reasoning. PsychRev 75.550–60.
HUTTENLOCHER, J., K. EISENBERG, and S. STRAUSS. 1968. Comprehension: Relation between perceived actor and logical subject. JVLVB 7.300–04.
HUTTENLOCHER, J., E. T. HIGGINS, C. MILLIGAN, and B. KAUFFMAN. 1970. The mystery of the 'negative equative' construction. JVLVB 9.334–41.
HUTTENLOCHER, J., and S. STRAUSS. 1968. Comprehension and a statement's relation to the situation it describes. JVLVB 7.527–30.

JOHNSON-LAIRD, P. N. 1967. Katz on analyticity. JL 3.82.

——. 1968a. The choice of the passive voice in a communicative task. BrJPsych 59.7–15.

——. 1968b. The interpretation of the passive voice. QJEP 20.69–73.

——. 1969a. On understanding logically complex sentences. QJEP 21.1–13.

——. 1969b. Reasoning with ambiguous sentences. BrJPsych 60.17–23.

——. 1969c. '&'. JL 6.111–14.

JONES, S. 1966a. The effect of a negative qualifier in an instruction. JVLVB 5.495–501.

——. 1966b. Decoding a deceptive instruction. BrJPsych 57.405–11.

——. 1968. Instructions, self-instructions and performance. QJEP 20.74–78.

——. 1970. Visual and verbal processes in problem-solving. Cognitive Psychology 1.201–14.

JUST, M. A., and P. A. CARPENTER. 1971. Comprehension of negation with quantification. JVLVB 10.244–53.

KATZ, J. J., and P. M. POSTAL. 1964. An integrated theory of linguistic descriptions. Cambridge, Mass., M.I.T. Press.

KLIMA, E. S. 1964. Negation in English. The structure of language, ed. by J. A. Fodor and J. J. Katz, pp. 232–46. Englewood Cliffs, N. J., Prentice-Hall.

KURODA, S. Y. 1968. English relativization and certain related problems. Lg 44.244–66.

LAKOFF, G. 1966. Stative adjectives and verbs in English. Mathematical linguistics and automatic translation. NSF–17.

——. 1971. On generative semantics. Semantics, ed. by D. D. Steinberg and L. A. Jakobovits. Cambridge, Cambridge University Press.

LEES, R. B. 1961. Grammatical analysis of the English comparative construction. Word 17.171–85.

LYONS, J. 1968. Introduction to theoretical linguistics. Cambridge, Cambridge University Press.

McCAWLEY, J. D. 1968. Lexical insertion in a transformational grammar without deep structure. Papers from the Fourth Regional Meeting of the Chicago Linguistic Society, pp. 71–80.

McKAY, J. C. 1968. Some generative rules for German time adverbials. Lg 44.25–50.

McMAHON, L. E. 1963. Grammatical analysis as part of understanding a sentence. Unpublished doctoral dissertation, Harvard University.

MEHLER, J. 1963. Some effects of grammatical transformations on the recall of English sentences. JVLVB 2.346–51.

MILLER, G. A. 1962. Some psychological studies of grammar. American Psychologist 17.748–62.

MILLER, G. A., and K. McKEAN. 1964. A chronometric study of some relations between sentences. QJEP 16.297–308.

PIAGET, J. 1921. Une forme verbale de la comparaison chez l'enfant. ArchPs 18.141–72.

——. 1928. Judgment and reasoning in the child. London, Paul Kegan.

POSTAL, P. M. 1970. On the surface verb 'remind'. Linguistic Inquiry 1.37–120.

ROSS, J. R. 1969. A proposed rule of tree-pruning. Modern studies in English; readings in transformational grammar, pp. 288–300, ed. by D. A. Reibel and S. A. Schane. Englewood Cliffs, N. J., Prentice-Hall.

SACHS, J. 1967. Recognition memory for syntactic and semantic aspects of connected discourse. Perception and Psychophysics 2.437–42.

SAVIN, H. B., and E. PERCHONOCK. 1965. Grammatical structure and the immediate recall of English sentences. JVLVB 4.348–53.

SEYMOUR, P. H. K. 1969. Response latencies in judgments of spatial location. BrJPsych 60.31–9.

SHIPLEY, W. C., E. D. NORRIS, and M. L. ROBERTS. 1946. The effect of changed polarity of set on decision time of affective judgments. JExPsych 36.237–43.

SINGER, M., W. G. CHASE, R. M. YOUNG, and H. H. CLARK. 1971. Practice effects in the comparison of sentences and pictures. Paper presented at Midwestern Psychological Association meetings, Chicago.

SLOBIN, D. I. 1966. Grammatical transformations and sentence comprehension in childhood and adulthood. JVLVB 5.219–27.

SMITH, C. S. 1961. A class of complex modifiers. Lg 37.342–65.

SMITH, K. H., and L. E. McMAHON. 1970. Understanding order information in sentences: Some recent work at Bell Laboratories. Advances in psycholinguistics, ed. by G. Flores d'Arcais and W. J. M. Levelt. Amsterdam, North Holland.

STAAL, J. F. 1968. 'And'. JL 4.79–81.

SVARTVIK, J. 1966. On voice in the English verb. The Hague, Mouton.

TANNENBAUM, P. H., and F. WILLIAMS. 1968. Generalization of active and passive sentences as a function of subject or object focus. JVLVB 7.246–50.

TELLER, P. 1969. Some discussion and extension of Manfred Bierwisch's work on German adjectivals. FL 5.185–217.

TRABASSO, T., H. ROLLINS, and E. SHAUGNESSY. 1971. Storage and verification stages in processing concepts. Cognitive Psychology 2.239–89.

TURNER, E. A., and R. ROMMETVEIT. 1968. The effects of focus of attention on storing and retrieving of active and passive voice sentences. JVLVB 7.243–8.

VENDLER, Z. 1967. Linguistics in philosophy. Ithaca, Cornell University Press.

WALES, R. J., and R. GRIEVE. 1969. What is so difficult about negation? Perception and Psychophysics 6.327–32.

WALLIS, C. P., and R. J. AUDLEY. 1964. Response instructions and the speed of relative judgments. II. Pitch discrimination. BrJPsych 55.133–42.

WASON, P. C. 1959. The processing of positive and negative information. QJEP 11.92–107.

——. 1961. Response to affirmative and negative binary statements. BrJPsych 52.133–42.

——. 1965. The contexts of plausible denial. JVLVB 4.7–11.

WASON, P. C., and S. JONES. 1963. Negatives: Denotation and connotation. BrJPsych 54.299–307.

WATT, W. C. 1970. On two hypotheses concerning psycholinguistics. Cognition and the development of language, ed. by J. R. Hayes. New York, Wiley.

WRIGHT, PATRICIA. 1969. Transformations and the understanding of sentences. L&S 12.156–66.

YOUNG, R., and W. G. CHASE. 1971. Additive stages in the comparison of sentences and pictures. Paper presented at Midwestern Psychological Association meetings, Chicago.